Practical ways to teach READING

Editor: Cliff Moon

Contributors: Linda Ashworth
Anne Baker
Shirley Paice
Sandra Smidt
Anne Thomas
Linnea Timson

 Ward Lock Educational

First published 1985 by
Ward Lock Educational
47 Marylebone Lane
London W1M 6AX

A member of the Ling Kee Group
Hong Kong · Taipei · Singapore · London · New York

British Library Cataloguing in Publication Data
Practical ways to teach : reading.
1. Reading (Elementary) — Great Britain
I. Title   II. Moon, Cliff
III. Ashworth, Linda
372.4'0941   LB1573

ISBN 0-7062-4568-7

Design by Hickey Press Limited
Printed by William Clowes Ltd, Beccles, Suffolk

Practical ways to teach
READING

Contents

To Margaret Meek

Acknowledgements

Acknowledgement is due to:

John Burningham and Jonathan Cape Ltd for the illustration and text from *Mr Grumpy's Outing* at the top of page 38.

Isao Honda and The Museum Press for the page from *Origami* on page 53.

David McKee and Andersen Press Limited for the illustration and text from *Not Now Bernard* on pages 31 to 33.

Foreword

It has been said that there are more publications concerned with 'reading' than all other areas of the primary school curriculum put together. So why another? If you analyse the authorship of books and articles on reading you will find that most are not written by practising teachers. All the contributors to this book either are, or have been until very recently, primary teachers.

Most of us were involved in a working group at the 1983 annual conference of the National Association for the Teaching of English at Guildford and we are all members of the national NATE Primary Committee. This book has arisen directly out of the feelings, ideas and practices which were aired both at that conference and in our regular committee meetings. Our theme is a series of descriptions of what it is like to teach reading in British primary schools in the mid-1980s against a background of almost revolutionary change in the way we think about the initial acquisition, and subsequent development, of the ability to read. These changes are outlined in the Introduction but they merely provide the rationale. It is the practical realization, the 'so what can we do?' question which occupies many teachers' minds at the moment.

The book's contributors tell you what they do but then leave you to decide how your own teaching might best develop along lines which will be appropriate for you and for the children you teach. They try to avoid prescription. Instead they *describe* their own teaching and pose questions which will enable you to examine your own.

So this book is essentially about practice and it is set out in a practical style. You are invited to use it as a 'workshop book', discussing its contents with colleagues, comparing notes and jointly planning the further development of the reading curriculum in your own school.

Cliff Moon, 1985

Introduction

Cliff Moon

As far as we can tell, it appears that at the present time the majority of British primary schools approach the teaching of reading in two main ways.

> They teach rules.
> They use reading schemes.

By *rules* I mean that infants or 'remedial' juniors are taught about phoneme-grapheme relationships and they are taught what is called a 'sight vocabulary' by means of flash cards or something similar. By *reading schemes* I mean that infant and junior schools use one, or more commonly several, published schemes through which their children have to progress before they are free to read books of their own choice. The contributors to this book, however, teach rather differently.

> They don't teach rules.
> They don't use reading schemes.

However, they are successful teachers and their children learn to read and to love reading. How can this be? Do developments in our understanding of the reading process support the way they teach? Why have they rejected the received wisdom of so many of their predecessors and contemporaries?

My task in this short introduction is to outline some of the developments and ideas which have culminated in these teachers' decisions to act as they do. The teachers who have written the chapters which follow describe what it is like to teach without a rule-based and scheme-based approach to reading. They tell you what they do instead and how the children respond to their alternative strategies.

Perhaps you teach rules and use a reading scheme. Perhaps you believe strongly in both and therefore feel that this book is not for you. I would still invite you to consider carefully what these teachers are saying so that you and your colleagues can decide at the end whether or not you might wish to adapt or develop your existing strategies in the light of what you have read.

In case you are growing more sceptical by the minute, it might be worth reflecting on something which was said during the Horizon film 'How Do You Read?' shown on BBC television in 1975. As far as I recall it went something like this:

> As long as there are children who learn to read without teaching, sometimes without recourse to books, often before they commence school, sometimes having never had a story read to them . . . as long as there are children like that, we cannot be certain that any method of teaching reading is the only or right way.

And there are such children!
And there are more than you may think!

A brief selective history of no-rule, no-scheme teaching of reading

1908

Huey said this of reading primers:

> No trouble has been taken to write what the child would naturally say about the subject in hand, nor indeed, to say *anything* connectedly or continuously, as even an adult would naturally talk about the subject.
>
> *The Psychology and Pedagogy of Reading*, p.279

1960s

Schools Council's *Breakthrough to Literacy* project confirmed that the most natural way to teach reading and writing was to use the child's own oral language experience. This 'language experience approach' has been successfully used with non-readers of *all* ages. It recognizes the relationship between learning to talk and learning to read and write which was emphasized by the Bullock Report in 1975.

1964

Kenneth Goodman started tape-recording poor readers and analysing the mis-match between what they read aloud and what the text said. He called these mis-matches *miscues* and later claimed that 'oral reading miscues were a window on the reading process at work'. He then developed a view of the reading process which emphasized the creativity of the reader. Readers, including beginners, bring an overwhelming amount of linguistic knowledge and experience to the task. Their miscues demonstrated this and showed that children could not possibly learn to read by a simple stimulus – response account of learning. Goodman continues to write and research. His work has been internationally acclaimed. (See F. Gollasch, *Language and Literacy: the collected writings of Kenneth S. Goodman*, Vols 1 & 2.)

1970

Brenda Thomson eventually published *Learning to Read* after a long struggle because she severely criticized every British reading scheme (most publishers had a vested interest in at least one!). She advocated the use of a wide range of carefully selected books, coded according to difficulty. Her teachers allowed children to interpret the meanings of books in their own words and to gain maximum enjoyment from them. According to the 1975 Horizon film every child who left her infant department could read.

1972

Frank Smith presented a psycholinguistic perspective on the reading process in a series of books between 1972 and 1983. He said that children should be encouraged to follow their natural inclination to make sense of what they read, rather than get trapped into word-by-word accuracy. He also said that the most difficult way to make reading easy was to be 'sensitive to what the child was trying to do'. (See F. Smith, *Reading*.)

1975

The Bullock Report, *A Language for Life* was published. The Report did not advocate any one method of teaching reading but it emphasized the link between oral and written language learning and experience. It also welcomed the initiative of those schools which were successfully organizing 'real books' instead of reading schemes as their chief literacy-learning resource.

1976

Margaret Spencer in 'Stories are for Telling' (*English in Education*, vol. 10, no. 1, p. 21) wrote this:

> The crucial difference between the present situation and any that has gone before is illustrated by the extraordinary pressure exerted upon children to become literate, and the incredible wealth of books for young children which exemplify, not the generality of pre-school experience, but the individuality and endless variety and vitality of storytelling. Yet the service of the latter is so little called on to advance the cause of the former. Our most pressing unsolved problem is to define and exemplify the place of children's literature in literacy.

1978

Margaret Donaldson published *Children's Minds* which was acclaimed as a superlative account of our current knowledge of how children learn. She traced the development of theories about how children learn to talk and read and concluded that behaviourist accounts were thoroughly out-dated. No one learns anything by first mastering rules or by learning sub-skills. We learn by trial and error and synthesis in meaningful contexts. Furthermore, learning which is not intrinsically rewarding is seldom sustained.

1979

Jill Bennett said in the introduction to her *Learning to Read with Picture Books* (p. 5) '. . . teach them to read by using *real* books (as opposed to "reading books") right from the start.' She described how she did this and went on to annotate over a hundred books which she found to be most helpful in her own infant classroom. An up-dated edition of her booklet is currently available.

1981

Gordon Wells published the results of the Bristol Language Development Project *Learning Through Interaction*, which had been carried out during the 1970s. As the title suggests, his books consolidated the interactionist view of language learning. That is, we learn to communicate within contexts which are meaningful and personally important to us. He went on to suggest that learning to read was not so fundamentally different from learning to talk. On page 272 he had this to say:

> . . . initial mastery of the skills of decoding is best achieved in the context of reconstructing meanings from texts that are interesting in themselves. But such texts must also be sufficiently close in content and form to the spoken utterances with which the child is familiar for him to be able to adopt strategies already developed for the comprehension of speech . . . . Alongside this runs a two-fold emphasis on possibilities inherent in spoken language, both of which prepare the child to cope with meaning in written text, but both of which are valuable in their own right. The first involves frequent reading aloud to children from a wide variety of written texts, so that they become increasingly familiar with 'the language of books' and better able to recognize the characteristic patterns of written text in the books that they read for themselves.

1981

Vera Southgate and her Schools Council research team published *Extending Beginning Reading* which had some strong things to say about the practice of hearing children read but was equally critical of the widespread use of reading schemes with 7–9 year-olds. Interviews with children revealed that few recognized the value of reading for current enjoyment. You learn to read in order to cope in secondary school and beyond into adult life. This disturbing trend is also evident in the interviews reported in the Assessment of Performance Unit's two Primary Language Surveys published by the DES in the early 1980s. Perhaps we ought seriously to examine what children are expected to read in school and *how* they are expected to read it, especially in view of what Margaret Donaldson said about intrinsic rewards.

1982

Bullock Revisited was published by the DES. Based on HMI observations and reports such as those of the APU, the pamphlet reflected on developments during the seven years since *A Language for Life* was published. As far as reading in primary schools was concerned there was general satisfaction with the standards of literacy achieved but the emphases for further development were on the encouragement of more extensive reading and an improvement in the teaching of literature.

1982

Margaret Meek published a book for parents called *Learning to Read*, but it is strongly recommended for teachers too! She based the book on four assumptions:

> - That reading is an important thing to do.
> - That reading is learned by reading.
> - That what the beginning reader reads makes all the difference to his view of reading.
> - That teaching and learning, to be successful, must be genuinely shared.

1982

Barrie Wade wrote a piece called 'Reading Rickets and the Uses of Story' in *English in Education*, vol. 16, no. 3. He contrasted the narrative structure and language of a Ladybird Reader and a John Burningham book, *The Snow*. He noted that it really made no difference whether you read the Ladybird text backwards or forwards and made this comment:

> It is not my intention here to criticize one particular reading scheme. I want instead to draw attention to the potential conflict in the minds of children caused by any reading which promotes arbitrariness instead of pattern, disconnection rather than coherence and emptiness rather than fulfilment. (p. 33)

Those three criteria, **pattern**, **coherence** and **fulfilment**, might be useful when selecting books for our classrooms. Wade concluded his article like this:

> I would criticize materials of the 'See Spot, Run Spot, Run' variety not only because, as Halliday says, they bear little relation to the language as a child has learned to use it. Additionally they make of narrative something apart from life as it is lived and they turn the food of story into a dry biscuit. (p. 36)

1983

Emilia Ferreiro and Ana Teberosky reported their Piagetian-style research findings in *Literacy Before Schooling*. They attempted to describe the stages through which young Argentinian children passed in their orientation towards literacy. When a child starts to read it is, in a sense, the end of a journey. Prior to that the child has conjectured about what reading and writing is for, what it is about and why it is all around them. You could say that this process must commence as soon as a baby's eyes can focus on objects like TV screens, cereal packets and so on.

When Ferreiro and Teberosky examined what happened during the first year of schooling (6–7 years in Argentina) they came up with a devastating conclusion. Children who were well advanced in their orientation towards an understanding of literacy made satisfactory progress with reading and writing. But those who were less well advanced were not helped by schooling – quite the reverse. The teaching they received actually frustrated their progress towards becoming literate. They were set back rather than further developed. Yet their more fortunate peers had achieved 'normal' development before they started school and without teaching. Why did this happen? The authors suggest that because the teaching of reading in Argentinian infant schools is rule-based the children were prevented from forming their own conjectures about print and testing them out by trial and error. And what kind of rule-based teaching are they talking about? Phonics and Look/Say methods! Ferreiro and Teberosky then admit that their findings may not apply to countries like Britain because teachers in more developed countries use more enlightened methods (like 'language experience') in teaching reading and writing. (See also Goelman, Oberg and Smith, *Awakening to Literacy*.)

1983

Shropshire County Council published a survey of reading teaching in its schools, *Reading Competence at 6 and 10*. Taken alongside *Literacy Before Schooling* the findings are deeply disturbing. Almost every infant teacher in the sample used rule-based approaches to beginning reading and only four out of forty teachers used a language-experience approach and even these four had no clear or informed view of the nature of such an approach. One teacher's comment illustrates the report's impact: 'I teach initial sounds, I don't know why. I suppose because you've got to teach something to start with. They can then attack the word.'

The report concluded that the theoretical base upon which most teachers were drawing was about thirty years out of date and that a substantial programme of in-service training was needed to bring the teaching of reading into line with developments in other areas of the primary curriculum.

The Shropshire Report of 1983 serves as a fitting conclusion to this brief history because teachers everywhere are now asking questions like these:

Are we the same as Shropshire?

and

If there is any truth in what
Literacy Before Schooling *says,*
What should we be doing?

The reading process

My first story

When I was a boy I was taught to swim by spending most of the lesson on the side of the pool practising arm and leg movements. The rest of the time was spent in the pool doing the same sort of thing.

I never did learn to swim during those lessons. Eventually a neighbour took me to the pool, coaxed me out to the middle, supported me, reassured me and helped me to trust my own buoyancy. Within a few weeks I could swim.

When I started teaching at Yatton Junior School in 1972 I had to teach my seven-year-olds to swim in our learner pool. The method was very different from my own early experience. The children were encouraged to jump, hop and splash about in the pool. They were given arm-bands and floats and most of them learned to swim. Of course their first width was something of a miracle. Few achieved it by anything that remotely resembled a conventional swimming stroke. After that they were shown more efficient ways of moving their arms and legs. Almost every child who left the school at eleven could swim well.

My second story

When my children had their first bicycles they had little wheels on each side of the back wheel. Even so I had to run up and down the road all Christmas Day holding their saddles and making sure they didn't wobble into hedges and gate-posts. Soon the little wheels were removed and then there was more saddle-holding until they could whisk along in a straight line, perfectly balanced. They didn't spend three months learning how to move their ankles, hold the handlebars and balance themselves in isolation from real bicycle riding.

My third story

One afternoon last summer we hired a small boat on the River Thames near our new home in Reading. All went well until we came to a lock. Although we had watched many boats negotiate locks on our walks along the river bank, this was the first time we had done it for ourselves. I can't describe our embarrassment as we lurched from one side to the other, hitting other boats and the lock sides. When the ordeal was over my wife said, 'But you've seen what other people do with the ropes — how they loop them around those posts and pay them out as the water drops.' She was right, of course, but what she failed to realize was that however much you see something demonstrated, however much you are told what to do, you only learn how to do it by having a go, getting it wrong and learning from the feedback your mistakes provide. Needless to say we returned via the same lock in perfect style!

Do you learn anything by learning the rules first?

What about board and card games?
What about self-assembly furniture?
What about learning to drive?
BUT is all that different from language learning?

1   Learning to talk

Years ago it was thought that young children learned to talk by imitating the words adults spoke to them and then receiving positive feedback for correct, and negative feedback for incorrect, repetitions. Obviously there is bound to be a degree of imitation in oral language learning because French children speak French, Chinese speak Chinese and so on. But it isn't anything like as simple as that because children of every nationality persist in using words and phrases which they *never* hear adults using. For example all English-speaking children go through a phase when they use two-word sentences like these:

Mummy car.
Daddy home.
Allgone milk.

Later, they over-generalize verb past tenses in sentences like these.

I goed to bed.
I rided my bike.

To begin with, these utterances provide evidence that children are not merely imitating but actively generating their own rules about how language operates. They are processing the data they infer from the language they hear around them. They are not passively receiving the data and reproducing them. Secondly, it used to be thought that children's 'incorrect' utterances were corrected by the adults around them because by the age of four or five most children were able to speak correctly, apart from the dialect forms which logically were bound to persist according to geographical, ethnic or social background.

The naturalistic data provided by the Bristol Language Development Project refutes this idea. *Parents do not correct their children's 'incorrect' utterances*. This is what they do instead. They respond to the utterance, they reply to it, extend it and take it further. In other words they *keep the conversation moving*.

When the child says 'Allgone milk', the mother might say 'Yes, that's right, there isn't any milk left and we'll have to go up to the shop to get some more, won't we?'

Another vital aspect of oral language learning is that it takes place in real-life situations where there is something important and interesting to talk about and where the other person has an important and often emotional relationship with the child.

What all recent studies of oral language acquisition have discovered is that children continually refine and expand their early undifferentiated utterances. They are not *taught* to do this. Their innate drive to communicate effectively enables them to process and re-process, conjecture, check and re-check their hypotheses about what to say, when to say it and how it should be said.

Is learning to talk all that different from learning to read and write?

2 Learning to read

A checklist

	Learning to Talk	Learning to Read
1 Are you taught the rules first?	NO	?
2 Do you get it 'right' at first?	NO	?
3 Do you learn from a scheme?	NO	?
4 Does someone correct your mistakes?	NO*	?
5 Are the things you communicate important and interesting to you?	YES	?
6 Is the person with whom you communicate important to you?	YES	?
7 Do you eventually become fluent and 'correct' by your own efforts?	YES	?
8 Are you allowed to learn from your own mistakes?	YES	?

Contrary to what many people think, the Bristol Language Development Project transcripts support this claim.

You could add further items to this list, drawing parallels between, and implications from, the two communication processes. It's a useful way of taking a fresh look at the reading process.

Of course there are differences and you are invited to add to the following table.

Differences between oral and written language

Oral	Written
Here and now	Another time/place
Informal	Formal
Aural signals	Visual signals
Low social status	High social status
Facing listener (except telephone)	Facing paper

However, the differences are chiefly concerned with surface form. They seldom impinge on deeper levels involving meaning or cognitive processes. *The way that speakers and listeners communicate is fundamentally the same as the way readers and writers do.* If we accept that position then what we do about reading and writing in school may be very different from what many teachers appear to be doing at the present time.

One further thought – *Do we read what we see?* Try reading today's newspaper aloud to a colleague. Did you read everything as it was printed? Did you make sense of it? Did your colleague notice when you read something differently from the way it was printed?

Most people admit 'interpreting' what they read in varying degrees and it is useful to reflect on why this should happen. In the same way as we are able to complete other people's sentences when they are talking to us, so we appear to impose meaning on what we read. We do not listen or read passively. We reconstruct the speaker's or author's meanings in the light of our own understanding and experience. So in a sense we do not read what we see but what we *want* to see or *expect* to see. Only when our expectations seem to be ill founded do we re-read, revise and move onto a different tack.

But does this only apply to fluent readers? The evidence from analysis of beginner readers' oral reading miscues suggests that *all* readers do this. We all bring a series of expectations to what we read right from the start as we shall see in what follows.

Scenario

A group of three- and four-year-olds who haven't started to 'read' yet are in a nursery classroom. They have a book corner and are used to thumbing through books, looking at the pictures and talking about them. There is a book of wild animals which shows a picture of a different animal on each page with a single word caption underneath. Here are the first few pages.

1 Elephant
2 Lion
3 Tiger
4 Crocodile
5 Giraffe

The teacher sets up a tape recorder and invites each child, in turn, to 'read' the book.

This is what happens

The children do two distinct things. The first group, the majority, say something like this:

> Once upon a time there was an elephant who lived in a forest. One day the elephant went out and met a lion. He said, 'Hello lion, shall we go for a walk?'
> 'Yes,' said the lion, so they walked along the path until they came to a tiger.
> The tiger went with them and . . . .

The second, smaller, group do these two things:

This is an elephant.		Here is an elephant.
This is a lion.		Here is a lion.
This is a tiger.	OR	Here is a tiger.
This is a crocodile.		Here is a crocodile.
This is a giraffe.		Here is a giraffe.

What expectations did the children have of the book?

The first group expected a story in conventional written form. The second group expected complete sentences in conventional written form.

You could say that all these three- and four-year-olds were far in advance of the designer of the book in their conceptualization of the book and the way it worked. The children were more sophisticated at both semantic and syntactic levels than the publisher supposed.

This scenario is a perfectly true account of what happened recently. It raises enormous questions about the kinds of books we provide for novice readers.

Which books do *you* know which would *match* a novice reader's expectations?

What are the negative effects on novice readers which could result from continually being faced with books which confound their expectations?

An introduction to each chapter

Chapter 1   Teaching infants to read

Linda Ashworth uses a language experience approach to the teaching of reading. She discusses her use of the Schools Council *Breakthrough to Literacy* resources. She also uses her children's oral language to produce home-made books which then become a reading resource for other children.

She frequently reads aloud to her children who have free access to a wide range of 'real' picture books. She describes how she organizes her classroom and how she monitors her children's progress.

Chapter 2   Developing reading with juniors

Anne Baker taught juniors in the same school as Linda Ashworth. She explains her thinking about the reading process and how this influences what she does in her classroom. Again she shows how children can be the authors of books which other children can read. Her long transcript of an extended reading session with Jonathan is an excellent example of the 'longer, less frequent pupil/teacher conferences' recommended by V. Southgate *et al* in *Extending Beginning Reading* (p. 321); it also highlights the collaborative learning which characterizes this chapter.

Chapter 3   Beginning to read

In one sense Anne Thomas extends and consolidates some of the issues raised in the first two chapters. However, an important point is that Anne frequently deals with children who have failed to make satisfactory progress in learning to read, yet her philosophy remains the same. In Margaret Meek's words, 'The best remedies are good teaching practice for all children.'

Chapter 4   Reading and our multi-cultural society

Sandra Smidt has wide experience in the field of multi-cultural education and she is involved in exciting innovative approaches to literacy learning in her school. She outlines the relevant issues and goes on to explain how she and her colleagues are putting into practice their respect for children's mother-tongue alongside the necessity to help them become fully literate in their second language. She describes how dual-language texts are being prepared and how they are used. She discusses organization and the relevance of her ideas to all schools and poses questions for further consideration.

Chapter 5   Reading and learning

Shirley Paice believes that two major problems are posed by young children's early contact with non-fiction. Firstly, most of the books written for them do not meet their needs; secondly, the children do not know how to use them. She explores these issues and describes how she attempts to overcome them in her infant classroom. She has liaised with a colleague to examine similar problems facing juniors and she concludes with a useful guide to selecting non-fiction for primary children.

Chapter 6   Literature for primary children

Linnea Timson responds to the *Bullock Revisited* statement that:

While it is recognized, then, that much has been done by schools to promote acquisition of the basic skills of reading, it is suggested that more needs to be done to promote the reading habit, that literature needs to be given greater attention in primary and middle schools than is often the case. (p. 9)

She outlines practical ways of promoting literature, includes a separate section on poetry and provides some useful criteria for selection as well as sources of further information.

Contributors

Linda Ashworth is Head of the Infant Department at Clifford Bridge Primary School, an open-plan school in Coventry. She recently completed the OU Language and Reading Diploma and is well known locally for her work in developing the Schools Council materials *Breakthrough to Literacy*. She reviews for *The School Librarian* and *Child Education* and has published articles in *Child Education* and local magazines.

Anne Baker has taught for eighteen years in primary and secondary schools and until last year taught juniors at an open-plan school, Clifford Bridge Primary, in Coventry. She now teaches at Courthouse Green School, Coventry. She is a member of NATE's Language and Gender Working Party and is a teacher member of the CNAA Language and Literacy Panel. She reviews for *The School Librarian*, has written for *English in Education* and has made a major contribution to *Children Reading to their Teacher* (NATE, 1984).

Cliff Moon taught in primary schools for seventeen years and is now Senior Lecturer in the Teaching of Reading at Bulmershe College of Higher Education, Reading. He reviews for several journals and has written books and articles on reading as well as a number of children's books. He is probably best known as the compiler of the 'Individualised Reading' lists of books published by the Centre for the Teaching of Reading at Reading University and as the editor of Books for Students' *Kaleidoscope* reading sets.

Shirley Paice has over eighteen years' teaching experience in junior and infant schools in Essex. She is currently Deputy Headteacher of Sunnymede Infant School, Billericay. Since studying for her Diploma in Reading, Language and the Curriculum she has specialized in young children's information books. She contributes articles and book reviews to various publications, including *The Times Educational Supplement* and *Child Education*.

Sandra Smidt is the head of William Patten Infants School in Hackney, London — a fairly typical inner city school which is working towards anti-racist and anti-sexist teaching and trying to implement a policy of teaching children to read through children's literature rather than through reading schemes. She was born and educated in South Africa and came to England in 1964. She taught for many years in Manchester, and read for an MEd at Manchester University (1977). She is currently trying – with the support of her staff – to combine being a headteacher with a full-time classroom teaching role.

Anne Thomas taught in a number of primary schools over a period of thirteen years before taking up an appointment as advisory teacher. She is now Head of the Language Development Unit at the Davidson Centre in Croydon. Her particular interests include reviewing children's fiction and teachers' reference books, encouraging teachers to be involved in classroom research and involving parents as partners in their children's education. She is well-known locally for her talks to teachers, students and parents on the topic of 'A natural approach: children as readers and writers'.

Linnea Timson taught in primary schools in inner city areas for many years, and is now Senior Lecturer (Language) at the Cornwall Education Centre. She has researched children's reading interests in East London and from 1977–81 was much involved in promoting and publishing books of stories and poems written by children in Newham. She is Book Review Editor of *NALEC Journal* (National Association of Language in Education Centres).

Teaching infants to read
Linda Ashworth

Introduction

I started teaching infants in 1966 and until 1969 I followed the well-trodden path of using flash cards and graded primers as my basic tools for the teaching of reading. My aim in those days was to produce fluent readers although, looking back, I was largely unaware of the nature of fluent reading. My short term objectives were to help each child climb the 'reading ladder' from 1a to 12c, using the *Ladybird Key Words Reading Scheme* and its support materials.

In 1970 I heard about *Breakthrough to Literacy*. I must have had reservations about the way I was teaching reading and been ready to change because the authors' manual revolutionized my views about initial literacy teaching. Since then I have been helping children learn to read and write using *Breakthrough to Literacy* materials and picture books. This chapter is about the ways children begin to read and write in my class.

When reception children come into my class I listen to them and observe them playing. Sometimes I use a tape recorder to record them talking: for example, in the Play House, where my presence would inhibit or change their use of language. Usually I just listen and note a few observations and conversations, like the following:

Matthew and Mark are playing with some 'Playpeople'.

Matthew: We're gonna play Star Wars. You be the prisoner and I'm not letting you out.

Mark: O.K. Help. Lemme out, lemme out.

These children are in the Play House.

Donna: You set the table.

Joanne: I am.

Lee: Woof woof.

Donna: Shut up dog or you won't get any dinner.

Rushma: You shut up. I'm reading the paper.

Diane and Katie are playing in the sand.

Diane: Let's make a seaside.

Katie: We'll do a sandcastle, a giant one.

Diane: Hey, look at this. It's going round. *(She is pouring dry sand into the sand wheel, thus making it turn.)*

Katie: It's the sand, look. Let's have a go.

Oral to written language

From such observations I assess the kinds of experiences the children have had before coming to school and the kinds of expertise they have gained.

Matthew and Mark are using language to play out a fantasy about Star Wars. The children in the Play House are aping their parents; using language to get things done, negotiating and responding. Katie and Diane are beginning to hypothesize about what is happening.

They are all expert talkers. Even Katie who is shy with adults, and Rushma, a second language learner, communicate freely and confidently with other children on the playground and in the Play House.

As the *Breakthrough to Literacy* authors say in the second edition of their Teacher's Manual, 'The child's own neighbourhood dialect may be the only resource they have for learning to read and write, and to present them with written language unrelated to this is to cut them off from their own experience.' (p. 10) This is why I introduce written language to children by using their talk as my prime resource.

Some children are ready to use written language when they come to school. Others need time to experience the school environment first. I rely on observation, listening and the attitudes and experience I have developed over the years to decide when to introduce written language to a child. This is how Lisa began to read and write.

Lisa was talking to me, while making a model.

Lisa: I mustn't get these shoes muddy.

Me: Why's that?

Lisa: Cus I'm wearing them to the wedding.

Me: Who's getting married then?

Lisa: My mum and I'm going to be the bridesmaid.

It was going to be the second marriage for Lisa's mother and Lisa wanted everyone to know about it. I asked her if she would like the news about the wedding written down for people to read. She thought that would be a good idea.

Me: What shall we say then?

Lisa: My mum's getting married and I'm going to be the bridesmaid.

Using the Teacher's Sentence Maker (*Breakthrough to Literacy* materials), I put the words she had spoken into a teacher's stand and said, 'What you've just said looks like this when it's written down. These are words. When we put some of them together it makes a sentence. Let's read what it says.' And we read it together.

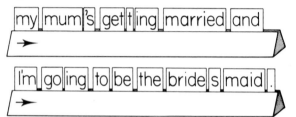

Most of the words we needed were in my central word bank but I had to make 'married' and 'bridesmaid'.

A conversation is often the starting point for me to introduce written language but sometimes a picture or model a child has made sparks off the need for a written comment. Gemma painted a picture of her cat with large hearts all over the paper. I asked her why she had painted all the hearts. 'I love cats,' she said. So this became her first written sentence.

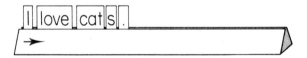

I often write these first sentences, made using the Teacher's Sentence Maker, into large books for everyone to share, although the sentences are made by different children. Sometimes I read the books aloud to the class. Sometimes children share them or look at them on their own in the reading area.

I could, like many infant teachers, merely act as a scribe, handwriting or typing children's comments, until they were able to write for themselves. Sylvia Ashton Warner used this method with Maori children as long ago as 1937 without any published materials, but I find the method very time-consuming and it makes children dependent on me. I use *Breakthrough to Literacy* materials which release my time and enable the children to be more independent.

When children have their own Pupil's Sentence

▲
Children sharing a teacher-made book.

▲
Child using sentence makers (playing with language).

Maker they can play with units of language: words, endings and punctuation, and move them around on the stand. This enables children to experiment with written language, just as they do with spoken language, before mastering handwriting and spelling.

Why 'Breakthrough'?

Breakthrough enables me to use the children's own language and therefore to fit the reading to the child, instead of fitting the child to the reading, as I used to when using a reading scheme. It gives children control over their own language development, because they make sentences about things which they find interesting. It also integrates the production and reception of written language because the first books children read are written or composed by themselves.

John had been at school about four weeks when I gave him his own sentence maker. These were the first sentences he made with it, so this was his first 'reading book'.

> the rocket is taking off into space.
>
> a flying saucer's landed.
>
> we made a big aircraft carrier.
>
> we haven't got a cat at school have we?
>
> the soldiers are fighting.
>
> we went to a show where some steam engines were.

John composed the sentences, I wrote them in his book and he illustrated them.

Most children are soon able to compose and read back complex sentences because the language structures are so familiar to them. This was Philip's second book.

> I like my dad because he takes me up to bed.
>
> the ghost is going up the stairs and it's scarey.
>
> my cousin had a hernia operation and yesterday he came to my house and he wasn't allowed to get excited so he didn't.
>
> I went to London to see some Daleks and I saw some trains too.
>
> I went to Hastings on a train and it was a long way and I was dying, then we got there.

Starting points

Children learn to read at different rates. Some begin very quickly because they have had a variety of experiences at home. Katie was ready to read and write when she came to school. She has lots of books at home which her parents often read *to* and *with* her. She belongs to a library and chooses books once a week while her mother chooses some for herself. She quickly found the reading area when she came into my class. She frequently chooses books to look at on her own, with a friend, or with me. She had her own sentence maker in her second week of school and loved to make sentences and read them. She shared Blake's *Mister Magnolia* and Knowles and Thompson's *Shirley Sharpeyes* with me during her first week at school and she was well on the way to becoming a reader after only a month at school.

Matthew, on the other hand, was not interested in written language when he came to school. He needed more time to play. He had to be shown by me what Katie already knew; that books can be as much fun as making models and painting. He is fascinated by Star Wars and space. So I have asked Scott, a junior boy with similar interests, to help. He was already writing a serial based on 'The Return of the Jedi', so I have asked him to simplify it and put it into book form. I shall type and 'publish' it. Scott has also offered to make an accompanying tape for Matthew. This approach might be the way into written language for Matthew, but he will make a slower start than Katie.

It was about two terms after Margaret started school that she had her own sentence maker. She takes much longer than most children to understand things and she seems to need more repetition in her sentences.

This is one of her books:

> my mum stays at home.
>
> grandma stays at home.
>
> I am at school.
>
> Julie is at school.

Speech written down

Using *Breakthrough* materials in this way, children learn that writing is their speech written down. Frank Smith, in *Reading from Process to Practice* edited by L. J. Chapman and P. Czerniewska (p. 106), points out that, 'Children must have two fundamental insights before they can learn to read

1 That print is meaningful.
2 That written language is different from speech.'

Language which relates to the child *is* purposeful, and if we use children's spoken language for their initial reading materials, then it can be written down as it was spoken. So the second insight can come later, when children have made a start with reading and writing. They gain experience of written language from the school environment and so the written language they compose becomes more like the 'book language' they hear adults read and less like talk. Georgina, for example, wrote the following after hearing me read Berenstein's *The Spooky Old Tree*, Nicoll and Pienkowski's *Meg and Mog* and Ahlberg's *Each Peach Pear Plum*.

This was the fifth book she had made and her experience of published books is beginning to show.

> I kiss Meg, do you dare - - - to go and buy a pear?
>
> Her mummy said,
>
> Go to bed.
>
> Do you dare?
>
> Yes.

One day long ago there lived a king and queen. And the queen wished for some children but she only had one.

◀ *Eleanor's version of Snow White*

Eleanor is six and an avid reader. This is how her version of Snow White begins.

> One day long ago there lived a king and queen and the queen wished for some children but she only had one. She was a girl called Snow White.

She often uses 'book language' like 'wished for' in her writing.

Published books

Alongside the use of children's own language as reading material, I use picture story books. I read my own favourites, often to the whole class. I show my enthusiasm for certain authors and stories in the hope that some of it will rub off on the children. It is no coincidence that all my favourites are story books. For me, as for Barbara Hardy in *The Cool Web*, edited by Meek *et al*, narrative is a 'primary act of mind' (pp. 12–13). Literature is a great motivator. Adults and children alike love a good story, so the vast majority of books in my school are fiction.

As well as reading to the children, I put many of their favourite stories on tape; I tape some and others are taped by older children for the younger ones to listen to. Children then have the opportunity to enjoy stories on their own or with friends, at times other than 'storytime'. Because I read the majority of our books to the children, they soon become familiar with the stories. Also, the *Breakthrough* printed vocabulary includes many of the hundred most-used words defined in McNally and Murray's *Key Words to Literacy* and since the children are already familiar

with these they are soon able to read simple picture books with surprising ease and obvious enjoyment.

Because I think choosing is an important part of reading, I encourage children to choose which books to read for themselves as soon as they start school. Some children, like Katie, already know how to choose. Most children learn quickly because of familiarity with the stories. They know which stories appeal to them and therefore which ones they want to enjoy again for themselves. Although we usually have only one copy of each title some are so popular that we have to have more than one. Particular favourites are Sendak's *Where the Wild Things Are*, Burningham's *Would You Rather?* and McKee's *Not Now Bernard*. If a child cannot choose a book, then I suggest a few titles and let the child browse through until a choice has been made. I also show children how to use the 'five finger test' to judge whether they will be able to cope with a book (see p. 17).

Which books?

Because I think choice is so important, I try to provide a range and quality of literature so that there is something for everyone. As I can never know what a child might need and when, I have to supply an extensive range so that the children are more likely to find what they want. The range includes myths, legends, fairy tales, classics, contemporary fiction, real life situations and fantasy. When I choose books for the classroom I have certain criteria in mind.

1 *My own enthusiasms are very important.* I don't enjoy reading aloud books that I don't like personally.

2 *The intrinsic value of the book comes next*. Is it a good story? Why has the author written it? That rules out most 'reading scheme' books where the story is often non-existent and the book has been written to 'teach' reading.

3 *Aesthetics probably come next*. Is it a beautiful book? Do the illustrations, the layout and the general presentation invite me in?

4 *Is the book relevant to the needs and interests of my children*? By that I don't simply mean is it about a familiar environment? I mean would it 'turn them on'?

5 *The language structures are very important*, particularly in books which children will be reading for themselves. If the structures are too artificial for the children to anticipate what might come next, like many reading primers, their meanings will be hindered.

6 *I also prefer books without stereotypes* of sex, race or social class. Bias can often mean omission of race, sex or social class other than the dominant, white, Caucasian, middle class, male. It can also mean tokenism, which is not much better (see chapter 4). Thus we have to choose carefully.

Although not all books I choose will meet all criteria, the best will. Books like Sendak's *Where the Wild Things Are*, Hutchins' *Rosie's Walk* and Carle's *The Very Hungry Caterpillar* speak for themselves. They show children the sheer delight books can give. Briggs' *The Snowman* is a wonderful book because it enables children of all ages and stages of reading to create their own fantasy around the pictures.

Book organization

It is no use, however, having a superb selection of books available, if children don't read them. They need to be accessible as well as available. I have already mentioned one way of making them accessible — reading them aloud to the children. Most of my books are displayed with covers showing, to invite children in. They are all within easy reach of small children. Children are also given the time, the freedom and the space to look at them whenever they want. The reading areas are all carpeted and equipped with easy chairs and cushions so that the children can be physically comfortable when reading or browsing.

I used to colour code the published books belonging to our school according to approximate readability levels. But our schools' library service books were left uncoded. We found, after a few years of this system, that children chose from the library service books simply what they liked, and did not seem as restricted as when choosing from our colour-coded books. Also their ability to read library books exceeded our expectations of what we thought they would be able to read.

Browsing through books in our reading area. ▲

Now we no longer try to grade books, other than by housing most of our very simple picture books together in one reading area (for example, Burningham's *Little Books*, Hutchins' *Rosie's Walk*, Berenstein's *The Spooky Old Tree* and *Breakthrough Little Books – yellow set*, Knowles *et al*), non-fiction in a second reading area and schools' library service books in a third. All the rest are together in the largest reading area.

I remember one five-year-old boy in my class being 'turned on' to reading and books in general by sharing Briggs' *Fungus the Bogeyman* with me. The 'readability level', had I assessed it, would have far exceeded Ben's reading ability. He couldn't read it all, but he was able to get from it what he needed.

Books written by children

I also shelve alongside publishers' editions, those 'published' by ourselves. These are written by the children or teachers, typed and put into book form by teachers, parents or work-experience students, and illustrated by the children, or by photographs, taken by ourselves. This was the first story Jody wrote for me to 'publish'.

A story about a little girl by Jody

Published by Ms Ashworth, Clifford Bridge Primary School, Coventry 1983. © Jody

About the author:
I am 5 and I have got long blonde hair and blue eyes. This is the first story I have ever written but I'm good at making dogs.

Once upon a time there was a little girl.
And the little girl got lost.
And she looked for some food.
And she looked and she looked and she looked and she looked.
Even if she looked and looked and looked, she still couldn't find any food.
The end.

Jody's first story

About the author.

I am 5 and I have got

long blonde hair and

blue eyes.

This is the first story

I have written, but I'm

good at making dogs.

Published by Ms. Ashworth
Clifford Bridge Primary School
Coventry, 1983.© Jody.

Two children wrote the next story together.

> ### Mog's Christmas by Amit and Lisa
>
> Mog didn't like Christmas because everyone was busy because they were all putting up decorations.
>
> Debbie said, 'I love Mog.' Then she told David and he said, 'I love Mog.' Then she told her mummy and daddy and they said, 'I love Mog.'
>
> Mog heard Debbie telling everyone, so she went off to see Debbie and she said, 'Would you like to play upstairs with a game?' 'Yes', said Mog, and it was Debbie's best game too.
>
> Mog was tired on Christmas day.
>
> The End.

They also listed, on the back page, all Judith Kerr's *Mog* books they could remember. Their mutual interest in cats and love of *Mog* books led to this joint project.

'Publishing' children's books in this way shows them that I value their writing, gives them an audience other than me, gives them an insight into being an author and, most importantly, provides a rich resource for others to read.

A time to read

A stimulating and inviting book environment is no good without the time to explore it. Children need time to browse, choose and read books from beginning to end, time to look at books on their own, with their friends and with teachers.

My school works an integrated day system, so that apart from hall times, which have to be time-tabled, children are free to look at books when they want to, during most of the school day. Also we begin every afternoon with a silent reading session of approximately fifteen minutes. When children come in from the playground, they each choose a small selection of books, and after registration we all browse, read books at length or just enjoy the pictures. I join in this activity by reading myself. Children aren't allowed to get up and change books during that fifteen minutes because we have found it too disturbing. We also have a shared reading session once a week, when children are encouraged to share enthusiasms with their friends, by reading books and discussing them with each other.

All children have 'reading with teacher' time, individually, once or twice a week, for about ten minutes each session. The content of these 'interviews' is varied and wide-ranging to suit each child's needs. I might read a short story book to a child who has just started school and, in so doing, show which way up books are read and that print usually goes from top left to bottom right. We might discuss different versions of a favourite fairy tale; which version the child likes best and why. I might talk about a new book a child's favourite author has written. Along with story time, when I read aloud to the whole group, and taped stories, when children listen to their favourite stories on tape, these 'reading interviews' give children an adult model for reading aloud and sharing a book. They also show children the strategies fluent readers use to make meaning from print.

Most of the reading my children do is on their own, with a teacher or with a friend or older child.

Teaching points

Sometimes though, there is a need to show children techniques in a large group or class; how to use a contents page and an index in an information book, for example, or how to follow instructions. I find it usually means more to the children if we do these things naturally, as the need arises, rather than creating an artificial need. Also, children understand better by making their own instructions and making a contents page and an index for one of their own books. For example, we made a photographic diary of the cooking we did for a recent Infant and Senior Citizens party. For this we made a contents page and an index.

Monitoring progress

In the days when I used a 'reading scheme' I used to monitor and assess children's progress by noting which books they were reading. I still keep a record of the books children read, and encourage them to take this over for themselves as soon as they are able to. Perhaps more importantly, though, I record their attitude to reading, the strategies they are using, their preferences and their own comments. I do this by systematically listening, observing and discussing their reading with the children themselves, with their parents and with my colleagues. Most of the assessment takes place during the individual reading interviews, but silent and shared reading sessions and short intensive observation periods are also tremendously valuable for this purpose. I encourage children to assess their own progress, both verbally in their reading interviews and in writing every Friday afternoon in a 'self-assessment' book.

A child's written comment in a self-assessment diary

> I liked reading to the reception class today. I read *The Tiger Who Came to Tea*. I like that story. I think my reading was brill this week.

Children not yet able to write comments can tape their comments or tell me what to write, or draw a symbol.

😊 = good, happy. 😐 = O.K. 😟 = stuck, sad.

If children are taking much longer than their peers to begin reading, I often tape their reading interview and listen at home, in order to analyse more closely what is happening. If parents want to help I sometimes make a tape of their child sharing a book with me so that they can hear the kinds of strategies I use.

In order to guide children in their choice of books I need to be aware of what is available. So I use the schools' library service, visit book exhibitions and read and write book reviews of children's books in publications such as *School Librarian*, *Child Education* and *NATE* and *UKRA* journals. We also run a school bookshop stocked by Books For Students (Berrington Road, Sydenham Estate, Leamington Spa, Warks.), which has a large self-service warehouse in Leamington soon to expand to larger premises in Warwick. This keeps us up to date with excellent, inexpensive paperbacks and encourages children to become book owners from an early age.

In the initial stages of reading and writing I rely heavily on *Breakthrough to Literacy* materials to facilitate the approach I use. But it is the *approach* that is important. If I didn't have the *Breakthrough* materials I would still use children's spoken language as an important resource for introducing them to print. I would just take more time to make every word a child wanted to use, instead of merely those not in the central *Breakthrough* word bank.

My aim is still to enable children to read fluently and critically, but more than that to show children the enjoyment that books can give, to get them 'hooked' on literature so that it can enrich their lives long after they have left school.

Further reading

Ashton-Warner, S., *Teacher*, Virago, 1980.

Hardy, B., 'Narrative as a Primary Act of Mind', in *The Cool Web*, edited by Margaret Meek, Bodley Head, 1977.

Smith, F., 'Making Sense of Reading and Reading Instruction', in *Reading from Process to Practice*, edited by J. Chapman and P. Czerniewska, Routledge and Kegan Paul, 1978.

The language experience approach I use is explained in more detail in:

Ashworth, L., *et al*, *A Practical Guide to Breakthrough to Literacy*, obtainable from Elmbank Teachers Centre, Mile Lane, Coventry.

Developing reading with juniors
Anne Baker

I teach seven–nine year olds and this chapter is about how I try to create a situation which makes it possible for children to love reading and come to value themselves as successful readers.

Learning to read

Several assumptions about the reading process underpin what I do. I assume that, like learning to talk, learning to read is a complex, developmental process, which involves children in change, both in relation to themselves and to the society in which they live. I assume that all the children I teach, from the slowest starter to the most fluent reader, are learning to read and will go on learning to read all their lives. I assume, too, that children learn to read by reading, by making sense of written language and that this, in itself, is a satisfying experience. I assume that children learn to read best in an atmosphere of mutual support and understanding, and of shared assessment.

My role as teacher

An important part of my role is to make available written language that is meaningful to the children and to help them get to know it by sharing it with them. Another important part of my role is to create time and space for the children to read on their own and to engage with other people in their reading, as well as in talking, writing and related activities, all of which generate reading and are themselves generated by reading. By working in this way with the children as individuals, in groups or as a class, I can come to understand their particular points of view, an important step if I am to enable them to develop as readers.

Written resources

I surround the children with print that I think will interest them. This takes the form of labels, notices, posters, maps and so on, as well as reference books, poetry and story books. Out of all the print available, the story books are indispensable. Stories hold a special fascination for children. They tell stories all the time and the 'let's pretend' of their play is similar to the 'let's suppose' of story. The focus of this chapter is, therefore, on stories.

So that each child will be more likely to find just what he or she wants when they need it, I aim to have as abundant a supply of as many different kinds of story as I can: modern and traditional fairy stories, folk tales, myths and legends, and so on, plus the children's own stories, published in book form.

Like mature readers, children need to range backwards and forwards as they read, so I make available picture and picture-story books, comic books, illustrated stories and stories with only a few, or no, illustrations interpersed in the text. Books like Briggs' *The Snowman* and Hutchins' *Rosie's Walk* have their place, therefore, whilst more demanding books like White's *Charlotte's Web* and BB's *The Little Grey Men* will extend the horizons of those who try to read them.

Criteria for choosing books

The right stories for children are those which give them most satisfaction, to which they return again and again. But I am also concerned that the children read stories that have the potential to enlarge their understanding of themselves, their relationships and the world in which they live. So, many of the stories I choose are by authors like Russell Hoban, Shirley Hughes and Catherine Storr, who not only tell engaging stories, but also relate powerfully and truthfully to the lives children lead. However, more than one child I know has been hooked into reading by Enid Blyton and other popular authors like Roger Hargreaves and Jim Slater, and by comics, so I allow books by these authors and also comics, even though I feel they sell children short in the stereotyped views they offer of people and the world.

A place to read

I try to make the reading area into a place that invites the children in to read, a place that is part of their living and working space, constantly accessible. Arranging the books in the reading area so that they look attractive and help the children find what they want is a way of valuing both books and children. I make use of a variety of display units and group picture-story books in one rack, the children's own stories in another, novels in an open case, taped stories and their texts on a bench, and so on. Wherever possible I turn book covers outwards to face the children. I don't grade the books. Books are to do with the meanings that are in the heads of the children who read them and I can't grade those.

So the reading area is attractive with books. It is also bright with plants, pictures and posters, curiosities such as shells and fossils, and with carpets, cushions, chairs and a settee, on which children can lie, or loll, or sit to read.

Mediating between children and books

The children are allowed to choose which books they want to read since they, more than anyone else, know what will have meaning for them. But I do what I can to help them choose, so that they can find the right book as quickly as possible. Early in the year I show the children where the books are in the reading area: the picture-story books, the novels, and so on, and by reading selections to them, indicate what they might find.

Throughout the early weeks and, indeed, the rest of the year, I spend time with individuals, groups and the whole class looking at books. I show the children a simple way of previewing a book by looking at the cover, title and author, and by flicking through it. We also examine books more thoroughly for details of front-page and back-cover blurb, copyright, publishers, dedications and contents pages. As children come to appreciate how books work, their power to use them grows.

I encourage the children to share their ideas on choosing a book which is about right for them. I demonstrate a simple 'readability' test they can use if they want to and we discuss different ways they might use the books they choose.

The five-finger test

If you feel a book may be too hard for you, do the five-finger test. Choose a page and begin to read it. Put your finger on any word you cannot read. If you run out of fingers on one hand before the end of the page, the book *may* be too hard for you.

If the book is too hard for you, you could look for another one that is easier. If you like it and want to read it all the same, ask someone to read it with you, a friend or your teacher. Or ask your teacher if you can take it home for your mum or dad, older brother or sister, to read it with you.

The following are some recommendations a colleague and I derived from conversations we had with our children, which were printed and duplicated for everyone to share.

Some ideas for choosing and using books

1 Choose a book to take to read to the Infant class.

2 Choose a book with your friend. Read it together and talk about it.

3 Choose a book that you already know. Books are often easier to read when you know the story first.

4 If you are reading a book of short stories, you don't have to read them in order. When you've finished one, go back to the contents page and choose another you think you will like. There is no need to read them all either. Just read as many as you want to then choose another book.

5 If you're reading a book and you find it gets boring, or too difficult, either finish it quickly and choose another, or change it at once.

Enthusing children

Children will only develop as readers if they want to read for themselves. To help them discover books as a source of pleasure, I share my love of books with them in several different ways.

I read aloud to the children at least twice a day, for a total of three-quarters of an hour, or more. In one of these sessions, a child reads, or I read, a complete story which is almost invariably a picture-story: a new one, an old favourite, or one of the children's own books illustrated by its author. The children help choose and it is very much a shared session, especially if the story is one we can all join in, like Dr Seuss' *The Sneetches*. This session is important because, apart from the delight it generates, it enables those children who cannot yet read the books for themselves to begin to do so, and it confirms to those who can read them confidently that picture-story books can, legitimately, be a continuing source of pleasure to them.

In the other session, I usually read a longer book in serial form, such as Edith Brill's *The Golden Bird*, or a story from a book of short stories, such as Amabel Williams-Ellis' *British Fairy Tales*. Again, the session is shared because the children like to talk about what has happened and the characters they have encountered; to compare their favourite passages and to wonder what will happen next. Although the books in this session are often too demanding, linguistically, for individual children to read, once children know how a story goes they are better prepared to read it for themselves.

I keep a collection of my own books, including my favourite children's stories, in the reading area for the children to borrow. I also encourage the children to buy books for themselves from the school bookshop. One of the most important things I do, is enlist the children's parents to share books with their children, for the sake of enjoyment; to come with them to the school bookshop and, if possible, to introduce them to a library.

Time for children to read

Children will only learn to read if they have the time to practise and find out, for themselves, what reading is all about. I give the children the opportunity to read every day, during an integrated-day structure, and I encourage them to use it. This, their time, is an occasion for much browsing, listening to taped stories, reading together and to each other, and talking about books, as well as sitting down to read a book on their own.

Three times a week, in addition to their own time to read, I invite the children to bring a book of their choice and sit down with me for half-an-hour's silent reading. I choose a book, too, and we all have the opportunity for a sustained period of reading without interruption. It is an important experience for us all. Those children who can tune into the 'voice' on the page quickly, do so and have the chance of getting lost in a book. Those who cannot yet cut themselves off from their friends to enter into the world of a book, have the chance to try, and also to see how more experienced readers go about it. Also, there is the chance to let the children see me read books for my own satisfaction. I can notice, too, those who find fulfilment in this activity and those who are still learning how to benefit from it.

Listening to children read

My long-term aim is to make it possible for children to become independent, autonomous readers. Thus, when I meet each child for a ten–twenty minute reading session, which I do as often as I am able, my aim is that we have a profitable but enjoyable time. During these meetings I share the book the child is reading and talk to him or her about it. I also like to ask children how they feel about their reading; to reflect with them on books they have read, or have had read to them since we last met; and, perhaps, look forward to their next book. But I try to be ready to respond to what the children are doing and to follow their initiatives. For example, as the children can choose what they read, I am never sure which book a child is going to bring to share with me. So I am prepared, if the book they bring is too demanding for them, to put them in touch with the text by reading it to them; or, if the book is an old favourite, to participate in their delight in being able to behave like an experienced reader; or, if it is more or less within their capabilities, to help them make sense of it.

I try to meet, every other day, those children who have made a slow start in their reading; those children who have some independence in reading I may see once a week; and confident readers once a fortnight. I find I can sit down with individual children while the rest of the class are reading, talking about books or otherwise engaged in their work. So that I can give my full attention to each child, I encourage the other children not to interrupt. It helps if I tape-record sessions, as children will usually tiptoe around me when a tape recorder is switched on. Tape-recording these sessions is useful, too, because by listening to the tape afterwards, I can reflect on what has happened during our reading and discussion, picking up nuances I may otherwise have missed.

Below and on the next three pages, you will find extracts from a transcript I made of a reading session with John. To make the transcript easier to understand, I have added notes in italics. The italic headings indicate what my general intentions were in each section of dialogue and the comments show more particularly what was happening within each section. Throughout the transcript: J = John and T = Teacher. The text we share is in bold type.

Transcript	Notes
How J. feels about his reading	
T: How are you getting on with your reading?	*It's important I take J.'s feelings and opinions into account right from the start so that he feels accepted as a partner in our dialogue.*
J: It's all right really because, um, I like it but when I come to big words, (T: Mm) um, I can't hardly read them and I have a guess (T: Mm) or I miss them out.	
T: I see. And do they stop you getting the story?	*I support J. throughout this to confirm his strategies. I want to be sure J. is focusing on what the text means.*
J: No not really.	
T: Not really. Anything else about your reading generally?	*An open question gives J. the opportunity to say whatever he feels is important to him.*
J: No.	

J. reflects on the books he's read

T: What have you been reading then? Let's have a look.

We are looking at J.'s reading card, a bookmark, on which he notes down each book he attempts. It is useful to refer to it in a reading session.

J: I read *Not Now Bernard* (T: Mm) that's quite, um, good (T: Mm?) I liked that book. And I liked *Tubby and the Poo-Bah* . . . .
and *Beano*.

J. tells me a little about this book he's enjoyed.

T: And *Beano*?

Comics are available. J. loves to relax with them, look at the pictures and figure out the text.

J: Yes. (We laugh)
T: You like that comic.
J: I like *Bears In The Night* quite well.
T: And *Bears In The Night*. You like that quite well do you?

I am now looking for the question that will help J. talk about what he's enjoyed.

J: Yes because I've read lots of the bear things. (T: Mm) *Bears In The Night, Bears On The Wheels*. I've read (T: Mm) *Bears' Christmas* (T: Oh, yes) *Bears With Scouts*. (T: Oh, I don't know that one.)

A genuine comment which allows J. to take the initiative and make this a genuinely shared experience. The book is actually called The Bear Scouts.

J: Um, they kind of go on their scout and they swing across this um ditch (T: Yes) this kind of river and (T: Yes) you see kind of ditch and he ties a rope on to a branch (T: Mm the dad?) and the boy ties a scout knot (T: Yes) the proper scout knot but the man the um dad ties a (?) he says it's a proper scout knot because he goes he wraps it round and then he wraps it round there and he swings across (T: Ha) and the wrap comes a-loose (T: Yes) and that wrap comes a-loose and he goes down into the ditch. Dead funny . . . .

In fact, J. rehearses the story for me, an important thing for any reader to do. The way he describes it shows his enjoyment. We discuss more bear books and J. agrees to pick out those he's read from the back of a Dr Seuss book and make a list for himself and for the class to share. We turn to the book he has brought with him, Robert the Rose Horse. *It is too long to read the whole book so J. decides to read his favourite bit with me. It is important that J. remains in control of the situation and makes the kinds of decisions he feels comfortable with.*

We share the book J. is reading

J: **Robert. The robbers ran right over Robert. They ran right over him and all they and away they went.**

J. miscues but corrects himself.

J. is reading quite hesitantly but with confidence and I try to give him an uninterrupted read . . . except for supportive comments.

T: Ooh yes.

J: They've ran over him look.

T: Mm knocked him flat. Poor old Robert.

Pictures and text are closely related.
I am concentrating on the book with J. and my comments show I am following the meaning and sharing in the enjoyment of the story.

J: **Robert got up fast. He had to stop those robbers. But how he could he did not he how could he do it?**

I don't interrupt and J. sorts out the meaning for himself.

     And then Robert saw a rose. It was not a big rose but it was a rose. Robert began to think. He began to th think he began to think faster.

T: What's he going to do?

Anticipating what's going to happen is an important part of reading, even if you've read a book before.

J: He's going to sniff the rose. So he'll do a big sniff and they'll go flat.

T: Ooh come on then.

I get involved in the story, partly to enthuse him, partly because I enjoy the story myself anyway!

J: **Robert went over to that rose. He put his nose right in that rose. He took a sniff, a big, big, sniff.** (J: sniffs) **and he began to get that old funny feeling. His eyes began to itch, his nose began to itch, then . . . .**

T: Wait for it.

As the climax approaches, J. becomes more fluent.

J: **Katchoo. Robert sneezed. Never was they a sneeze like it. Away went cats. Away went hats. Up went dogs, down went birds. Bang went the guns. Up went the black bag and Robert fell down flat.** (T: Yes) **Look** (T: Yes) the dog's holding on to the lamp post.

T: Mm and these people look.

J: Look and the birds 's falling down to the floor . . . .

We complete the text and both agree we enjoyed it and I leave him to read it again for himself.

We look forward to J.'s next book

T: And what do you think you'll read after this? What have you a fancy for next?

J: *The Best Nest.*

T: *The Best Nest.* And what makes you want to choose that?

It's important that I support J. in his choice. I am not asking, here, to criticize.

J: Because it's good because I've read it once.

T: You've read it once have you already?

J: Mm.

T: Do you like reading books several times over and over again?

I feel J. is keen on reading books over and over again, some till he knows them off by heart; an important stage in a reader's life — hence the question.

J: Yes because I get the story first I get, um, kind of the story (?) then I then I really read it.

T: Then you really read it and it takes a couple of goes perhaps to get into it does it?

J: Yes.

T: And you get the story first (J: Mm) and then (J: I really) you really get into it.

J: Yes.

T: Mm well I wish you luck with your reading. OK, thank you very much.

What J. says he does, here, seems crucial to me. Later, when he meets unknown texts, such as novels, his capacity to give himself time to get into a book will be important.

Notes towards a profile

To preserve the memory of reading sessions and to build a profile of my children as readers for them, their parents and myself, I keep notes about each session. Sometimes I write down verbatim what children say during their session and perhaps remind them of what they have said at a later date so that they can make comparisons, reflect on ways they are growing and changing, and also see the point of the notes. But mostly I make the notes after the sessions have ended. What I wrote after the taped reading session with John appears below.

J. finds reading all right, likes it. Guesses or misses out big words. They don't interrupt the story for him. Still into Dr Seuss and comics. Has read lots of Berenstain bear books. Told me about *The Bear Scouts.* Very enthusiastic. Going to make a list of them for 'self and the class to share. Must remind him I've got *The Berenstain Bear's New Baby* as he didn't mention that. Shared *Robert the Rose Horse.* Has read it before. Told me about his favourite bit. Chose to read that. Resuméed book to that point. Reads hesitantly but confidently for meaning. Corrects 'self. Sorts 'self out. Uninterrupted read. Uses the pictures. Going to read *The Best Nest* next. Reads books once to get into the story, then again. Enjoyed the session.

Responses to reading

Talk arises spontaneously when children read and share books, and writing and art are generated. So that children are aware of the possibilities of ways of expressing responses to their reading, I spend time discussing with them what they might do when they have read books they have enjoyed. The following list of ideas grew out of one such discussion and was developed into a poster for everyone to share.

What you can do when you have read a good book

1 Read the book again or one like it.
2 Read another book by the same author.
3 Share the book with a friend and talk about it.
4 Tape the story for others to listen to.
5 Make a poster advertising the book.
6 Include it in your list of favourite books.
7 Write a letter to the author.
8 Write a book review for the reading area.
9 Paint a picture of your favourite character or scene.
10 Act out the story, or your favourite part, with your friends.

Talking about books

When children talk together about the stories they have read, they think out loud and find out what they mean. Talking helps them to sort out their ideas. I encourage them in this and give them opportunities to talk, but I also want the children to have the confidence to share the experiences of others by listening.

Here is a short extract from a transcript of a tape of two children talking about a book they have both read. They weave their thoughts and feelings together, not in the language of evaluation, but in their own language, infused with the language of the book. Their involvement in and enjoyment of the story show powerfully through their responses.

How Tom beat Captain Najork

a transcript

M = Michael, *P* = Paul

M: I like that bit at the beginning when she's singing and the bird faints (P. Yes) off the tree and when she starts singing all the flowers die.

P: He fools around with sticks and stones crumpled paper mewses and passages dustbins. I like that when he's (?) (M. Yes) broken bent nails broken glass and holes in fences and mud. He stamped and squelched and slithered through it

M: and he pulled things out the rivers

P: and played around with ladders and high things that shook and wobbled and teetered. (M. Yes) (?) playing with barrels

M: and er he played with old bottles and muck

P: things up high and things down low

M: yes and

P: eat your greasy bloaters.

M: It's a good book isn't it?

Writing about books

It is important when children write as a response to reading a book that their communication is a genuine one, that they write because they want to and for a real audience. One of the many things children can do is write to the author of a book they have read and then wait for a reply. When a reply comes the children discover authors as real people and some of the mystery of the 'voice' on the page is dispelled.

Here is a letter Rifat wrote to Catherine Storr and to which she received a very satisfying reply.

Clifford Bridge School.
Coombe Park Road.
Binley,
Coventry.

Dear Catherine Storr,

I enjoy your Polly books. They are my favourite because they show you how to trick a wolf's mind if you meet a wolf. They also tell you to keep a pie, a chocolate cake and a pot of toffee handy in case some hungry wolf does come along. Polly and the Stupid wolf is my favourite because it is the most exciting and my favourite story is Little Polly Riding Hood because its the funniest and because Polly tricks the wolf the most. My little sister has seen the books and she enjoys them as well.
Please tell me where you got the ideas of Polly and the wolf from. Why is Polly so clever and the wolf so stupid? And why are Clever Polly And The Stupid Wolf and Polly and the Wolf Again published in 1955 and 1957 when Tales Of Polly And The Hungry Wolf is published so much later?
Please may I have a list of books you have written so I can try them? And can I have your autograph please?

Yours sincerely,
Rifat Sahi (age 8)

Children's own stories

The children write stories, or tell stories and have them transcribed, all the time. Their own stories are an important part of what is available for the children to read. When they are finished they are typed up and published by me, with their authors' permission, and their authors illustrate them. Then they are given to the person for whom they were intended or they are placed alongside commercially produced books for everyone to read. They are significant because, for one thing, they are good stories. Also, their authors know their texts and can read them confidently and share them with others. Telling and writing their own stories, and having them published demystifies the world of printed stories because the children can see that what they are doing is of the same order as the authors they read; books are not just something done to them by others, but something they can do for others. It also confirms to the children that their own language is accepted and valued.

Most children tell or write a story because they have one in their heads. Quite often their story is an indirect response to what they have read. Diane, newly independent in reading and writing, decided she wanted to write a novel. She wrote it in a little notebook, a chapter at a time, over a period of two weeks. When she had finished, she read it with me very carefully to make sure she had said exactly what she wanted to say. Then, with her permission, I edited it and published it in book form for other children to read.

THE MAGIC SWEET THAT DONNA ATE

by Diane

Published by Clifford Bridge School.
Copyright 1982 Diane H_____ .
No part of this book may be copied without the permission of the author.

ABOUT THE AUTHOR

I write a lot of books. I have been doing books for 2 years or more. I have a sister and a brother and a dog. And my sister's name is Sarah and my brother's name is James and my dog's name is Sandy.

THE MAGIC SWEET

One day a little girl called Donna went home from school and she found some sweets. And on one of the sweets it said, 'Eat Me,' so she did. And she started to grow bigger and bigger, bigger and bigger until she wanted to go outside. So she bent down and got a key what was on a table.

And she got the key and she wanted to go through the door. And she cried and cried, cried, cried, cried, cried, cried. And she found a bottle with a label. And it said on the label, 'Drink Me,' and so she did. And she shrank and she could get in the door. And when she got in, there was another door and another door and two more doors.

And on the last door she went through there was a lovely garden and flowers. And she could not believe her eyes when she looked at all of the things that were in the garden. And she even saw some of her favourite birds when she was in the garden. And she fainted. And some little men caught her and took her to their home.

The little men caught her and took her to their home. When she woke up she said to the men, 'Leave me alone.'

'No, no, no, no, no, no, no, no, no, no.'

'Leave me alone.'

'Parlez-vous Anglais?'

'Pardon? What did you say?'

'I do not know the meaning of the word. Never mind. Let me go.'

'No, no.'

'Yes.'

'No.'

'Yes.'

'No.'

'Yes.' And on until she was free to go. And she ran and ran and ran as fast as her little legs would take. And she remembered the key and she got the key out of her pocket. And it was not there but she had it in her other pocket and she was glad.

And she had it in her other pocket and she was glad that it was in her pocket. And she took it out of her other pocket and she opened the door. And outside was Nichola.

'Nichola, how did you get here?'

'The same as you did.'

'What, down that big hole?'

'Yes.'

'I should not go in there,' Donna said. 'There are two men who catch you and take you into their house.'

'Oh, I won't go in then. We better be going home.'

'We can't go up the big hole.'

'We cannot go up the big, big, big hole,' said Donna.

'Yes, we can,' said Nichola.

'How?'

'Easy. When I fell down I brought some rope to get you and me out.'

'So we can go home?'

'Yes, we can.'

'I am glad.'

'So am I.' So they went home.

'What a lovely dinner, Mum,' said Donna. 'I have had a lovely adventure.'

'Shut up,' said Dad.

'Dad, please can I tell you my adventure?'

'All right then.'

'I was on my way home from school and I fell down a hole, a big, big hole. And there was a bottle and on the bottle it said, "Drink Me," and on a key it said, "Eat Me," And then that is all I can remember.'

THE END

I speculate that Diane's story somehow mirrors symbolically her inner feelings but, whatever the motivation, it is certain that in her writing she drew on the rich supply of stories that have been read to her and that she has read to herself. Features taken from stories, which she transforms and makes her own, include magic sweets and potions, a bottle with 'Drink Me' written on the label, a child who grows big and shrinks small, and little men. Throughout her story, she has fun and plays with words as in the repetitions of 'cried' and in the exchanges between Donna and the little men. And Diane shows a fascination for form in her use of chapters. She even invents markers to show the end of one chapter and the beginning of the next. Her language is a mixture of book-language and the way she talks. Like many children she imposes on her story features that are unpredictable, such as the curious response of Donna's father towards the end.

The children's own records

The children are asked to be responsible for keeping a list of the books they read on a reading card. This serves as a bookmark and as a focus for discussion during reading sessions. At the end of each week the children transfer what they have read during the week on to a reading record. They enjoy doing this and also looking back to remind themselves what books they have read, and how many. The reading record serves the children, their parents and myself, as it builds to show the balance and pattern of their reading; the range of books they enjoy and books they do not like; the nature of the challenges they have set themselves and where they go for a quick, comfortable read and reassurance. The reading record is also useful as a focus for the conversations the children have about books. They like to pick their favourite books out of the record to talk about with their friends. Here is the reading record Jane kept over half a term.

Reading Record of Jane 1982/3		
Date	Title	5 star rating or comment
14.1.83.	*Grey Rabbit and the Wandering Hedgehog*	O.K.
	The Twits	O.K.
	Merrymole	fab
	Casey, the Utterly Impossible Horse	ace
21.1.83.	*Story Teller*	ace wish I had it
	Early One Morning	O.K.
	The Owl Who Was Afraid of the Dark	fab
	The Little Match Girl	O.K.
	Animals	*****
4.2.83.	*And I Mean It Stanley*	*****
	The Snowman	O.K.
	Laura and the Bandits	O.K.
	The Witch Next Door	O.K.
	The Shrinking of Treehorn	fab
11.2.83.	*Jenny and the Cat Club*	fab
	Story Teller 3	fab
	Paddington's Garden	fab
	Helen's Story Teller	fab

Jane's record shows that her choice ranges through picture-story books, books of short stories, novels and taped stories with their texts. She includes in her choice stories selected and taped by another child in the class, Helen. She mentions only one book of non-fiction. Her autonomy in choosing books allows her to create her own pattern of reading which is valid because it is hers.

The children's self-assessment

At the beginning of a school year I invite the children to keep a journal in which they write each week to share with me an assessment of their thoughts and feelings about their work. Asking for their own evaluation of themselves offers the children a new perspective on their learning. My response to their thoughts is in writing and, gradually, over the year a written dialogue develops between the children and myself.

On the following page are extracts from the journal Antony kept which represent something of what he thought and felt about reading over a whole term.

Extracts from Antony's journal

I do enjoy storys lik Jack and the Giant Killer I liked that story I like that kind of work doing reading.

I will Try the Books on Wizards I like the Book about Witches I liket the Books by Dr Suess Very very much like How the Grinch Stole Christmas and off course the lorax and Snetchers and oh the thinks you can think and Old Hat New Hat.

I enjoy reading and writing, then Maths, I like reading Dinosaur books very very very much, and alos i like very very much is history books, my dad has got a history of England. I read it and i like reading it to, so has my old friends dad. he has got history of the world.

I will try to find the library, you think is best for me, ... I think I worked harder this week for writing and for reading two, I am going to town on Saturday.

I went to the library and i got some good books, the Secret Seven, and a book of stories, a Book of Ghosts, and Witches and the Phoenix and the Carpet.

Is there a Secret Seven book in the reading area. Well I would like to read them.

I bought a Secret Seven Book, on this Monday called the Secret Seven and I have ordered a Joke book, when I bought the Secret Seven at the bookshop.

By keeping his journal, Antony learned a lot about himself, about the right books for him and where to find them and about his reading during the term. By reading what he had written I was able to keep in touch with his approach to reading and what it was like for him. By responding, in writing, to his thoughts and feelings I was able to acknowledge what he was doing in his reading, to direct him towards books he wanted to read and to confirm him as an autonomous reader.

Conclusion

Not so long ago, I tried to develop reading by first teaching children to read using reading-scheme books, exercises and tests and then letting them go on to 'real' books. Though some children found it easy to read 'real' books when they got to them, many found the transition from the initial teaching process to 'real' books difficult, if not impossible, to negotiate. For some children it was as if they had to learn to read all over again.

Gradually, by talking to children about their reading, by thinking about what the 'experts' said (especially people like Connie and Harold Rosen, Frank Smith and Margaret Meek) and by discussing reading with other teachers, I came to understand reading as a developmental language process, and to recognize the power of children to learn for themselves and to collaborate with others in their learning. I came to appreciate the part meaningful stories play in motivating children to read and in teaching them the lessons of reading. I also came to see myself not so much as a teacher but as an enabler — one who makes learning possible. What I have learned is that developing reading is a complex of interactions between stories, children and their teacher. What I have attempted to share in this chapter is the outcome of that learning.

Questions to think about

1 What kind of reading experiences do you enjoy?
   What kind of reading experiences do you want for your children?

2 How did you learn to read?
   What kind of progress have you made in reading?
   Is there any conflict between how you think you learned to read and how you progressed and the practices which are followed in many schools?

3 What kind of books have you enjoyed throughout your life?
   Is there any difference between the books you enjoyed for yourself and those books you were required to read in schools?

4 Who taught you that stories are to be read for enjoyment?

Who taught you that it is important to read to the end of a story?

Who taught you how pictures and text work together in a picture-story book?

Who taught you what to expect of a novel?

5 What kinds of stories do your children most enjoy? Are these the same stories your children are learning to read with?

6 What kind of progress in reading do your children make?

Can reading 'easy' books be a sign of progress?

How do you measure progress when children read more demanding books?

7 How do you assess children's reading?

What do your children have to say about their reading?

Beginning to read

Anne Thomas

'To learn to read, children need the attention of one patient adult, or an older child, for long enough to read something that pleases them both. A book, a person, and shared enjoyment; these are the conditions of success.'
Margaret Meek: *Learning to Read* (p. 9)

It is becoming apparent that most of the children in our primary classrooms will learn to read despite what we, as teachers, do or do not do. This comment is not designed to create complacency, but it can serve as a basis for reflecting on the theories and practices that pervade the whole area of language learning and teaching in our schools.

How children actually learn to read remains a mystery. What we do know is that many learn with amazing ease, while for some the task seems almost insurmountable. It is this dichotomy that forms the basis for a series of discussion points and activities in this chapter.

How do we teach reading and what do we think is involved?

All teachers are teachers of reading and as such we need to reflect continually on our teaching strategies and the philosophies that underpin them. How can this best be done, when we consider the thousand and one other demands that are made on our time during the school day? The simple answer is to suggest adopting a more relaxed and reflective approach to classroom interaction; shift our approach from behaving like a teacher to behaving like a learner. We could adopt the attitude that learning is a collaborative activity whereby we learn alongside others: exchanging ideas, formulating new concepts and subsequently applying them in a variety of situations.

We all have expectations of what a child needs to know in order to learn but these expectations do not always converge with those of the child. This statement is the one that enabled me to question my own approach to teaching children who were finding learning to read difficult. Hitherto I had considered that because certain children were not making headway I had to employ a more carefully structured stage-by-stage programme. In one instance with a meticulously planned phonic programme by my side I

set about teaching a particular child a sound at a time. This was done in isolation from any kind of shared story reading. It dawned on me after some months that the kind of transference that I was expecting was not being realized. The child, during these sessions, was becoming more and more confused and developing a negative view of himself as a reader. Yet this same child when listening to a peer reading a story aloud continually anticipated the text for her. How could he do this?

Here is one more example from an early experience. A child reading from a reading scheme book, came across this sentence: 'The bee bit the boy on the nose.' He read it correctly, albeit with a note of disbelief. 'Why doesn't it say "stung"?' he interjected. The compilers of this book, in their effort to make learning to read easier (by over-simplifying linguistic structures and conforming to certain beliefs about controlled vocabulary and phonic analysis) had in fact created a situation whereby the learner was unable to draw upon his greatest strength: a well-developed knowledge of language in use.

These occurrences and others like them brought about a feeling of unease and doubt. Hitherto I believed that reading methodology involved teaching a set of discrete skills; if children were finding the activity difficult then the process must be fragmented. But, in practice, I discovered that much of the teaching that is involved in the 'look and say' and phonic methods seemed to be counter-productive and unrelated to the child's natural urge to make sense of all learning situations. Children do not learn to talk by being taught one word at a time or a sound a day; they learn to talk through successful interaction with others. Meanings are exchanged in wholes, not in isolated fragments.

If learning to read is analogous to learning to talk, how does that affect the way we think about the teaching/learning of reading?

Selecting materials to support the emergent reader and writer

The majority of reading schemes or programmes to be found in our schools are based on the idea that reading is primarily a perceptual process, where the visual and auditory aspects of orthography have to be learnt before you can read a continuous and meaningful text.

Both aspects are fraught with difficulty. How long would it take to learn to read if it were necessary to be able to recognize all the so-called 'irregular' words by their respective configurations? Similarly, if the phonic approach were strictly adhered to, consider the tedium and frustration that would be brought to bear on the learning situation. These kinds of skills are ones that develop while a child is learning to read, not before.

Discussion point

How far do the most fundamental aspects of learning to read evolve from the learner's willingness to:

1 use his/her knowledge of language to anticipate, predict, hypothesize, confirm or reject?

2 enjoy and share a story?

3 be involved in making the text meaningful?

4 feel that learning to read is a worthwhile and valuable activity?

In addition, how can we create the kind of learning environment that would facilitate these kinds of opportunities?

One of the basic differences between a reading scheme book and a story book for children is that the former is devised chiefly for the purpose of teaching certain discrete skills while the latter is written to engage children in the magic of story for its own sake. Many reading schemes seem to lack, particularly in the early stage, an acknowledgement of children's prolific knowlege of how language works and of how stories work. Learning to read becomes difficult when these two factors are ignored. Thus, if children are to draw and build on what they already know, are there ways in which these obvious strengths can be utilized to good effect?

Children as readers and writers

Imagine a group of four, young, first-year juniors. They are all at the beginning stages of learning to read. Not one of them is confident. They do not see themselves as potential readers. Reading for them is synonymous with disenchantment and potential failure. However they could all recall and tell a story. The following plan was put into operation:

1 Two stories were read to the children – both involving a magic pot; one originated in Italy, the other in the Caribbean.

2 The children were invited to tell, or talk about any other stories they knew based on this theme.

3 They were invited to make up a similar story as a collaborative venture.

4 They were given a tape-recorder, a quiet corner and time.

The following is a transcription of their story.

Super Granny Rebecca and the Magic Pot

Super Granny Rebecca lived in a little cottage in the woods and she had a magic pot. She used to cook –

bananas on Monday,

onions on Tuesday,

baked beans on Wednesday,

spaghetti on Thursday,

sticky jam on Friday,

biscuits on Saturday and on

Sunday she made a lot of stew all in her magic pot.

Page 2

One Sunday Kevin Alex was lost on his bike in the woods. All of a sudden he saw a little cottage but he did not know who lived there. He was scared but he knocked on the door and called out, 'Is anybody there?'

He heard a tiny croaky voice say, 'Who is it?'

Page 3

'My name is Kevin Alex and I am lost in the woods. Can you let me in please?'

Super Granny Rebecca opened the door and said, 'Come in dear Kevin Alex.'

As he went in he could see some meat, onions and potatoes waiting to be cooked.

Page 4

Super Granny put the food into the pot while Kevin Alex went into the woods and picked flowers for her. So he could not hear her say,

'Magic pot, magic pot.
Make me some food.
That's nice and hot.'

Page 5

So when Kevin Alex came back from the woods with his flowers the pot was bubbling away on the stove — very hot.

'Do you want to stay for dinner and for a couple of nights?' asked Super Granny.

Kevin Alex was very, very pleased and said thank you.

Very quietly Super Granny Rebecca said these magic words,

'Magic pot, magic pot,
Stop, stop,
Before it's too hot.'

Page 6

After dinner Super Granny told Kevin Alex that she must go to the woods to pick some strawberries.

'While I am out please do not touch my magic pot or
    something
        TERRIBLE
            will
                happen.'

Page 7

Super Granny Rebecca went out of the back door to collect some strawberries.

On the floor of the cottage was a book. Kevin picked it up, turned the pages over until he got to page 10. There were the magic words. He read them aloud,

'Magic pot, magic pot,
Make me some food
That's nice and hot.'

Page 8

As he said the magic words the pot started bubbling. The stew began to rise up and soon it overflowed.

It slithered across the kitchen floor, out of the windows and doors. It filled the village street — even knocking trees down on its way.

Page 9

Super Granny flying home on her broomstick saw the stew everywhere.
Quickly she said the magic words,

'Magic pot, magic pot,
Stop, stop,
Before it's too hot.'

The magic pot stopped — just in time — before it reached the last of the villages.

Page 10

Kevin Alex was stuck in the middle of the stew in the cottage.
When Super Granny was able to free him she gave him a spoon and told him to eat all the stew.
for ever
and ever
and ever . . . .

Scripts were typed for the group and put together to make individual books. Each child designed a book cover, and illustrated each page, having discussed the importance of matching picture to text.

What did the children already know about story and about written language?

1 That a complete story has a beginning, a middle and an end.
2 That written language is different from spoken language.
3 That story is 'disembedded' language and as such the reader must be given all relevant information. (Written language needs to be self-explanatory.)
4 That the sequences of story must link one with the other to create a coherent whole.
5 That this type of story has its own particular patterns of language.

What other benefits accrued from this activity?

1 The children were able to behave as real readers and writers.
2 They had a tape recording of their story which they could listen to and enjoy.
3 The text was a 'known' text so they could all soon read the story for themselves. (They could match what was in their heads with what was on the page.)
4 They had written a book which others in their class would enjoy reading.
5 They had begun to believe in themselves as potential readers, writers and, most importantly, as viable learners.
6 This was a real story using real language.

How can you do this?

Invite groups of children in your class to collaborate in creating stories. Provide some kind of stimulus and then observe how they work together to achieve their objective.

Listening to and observing children as they read aloud: what can we learn?

Listening to a child read aloud is so much more than simply noting what he or she cannot yet do. The prime consideration is that the encounter should be enjoyable and worthwhile: both the teacher and the child are working in partnership.

What you need: a child, a book, a tape recorder, uninterrupted time and a reasonably quiet and comfortable situation.

What you do: 1 Invite the child to read to you from a self chosen and familiar book.
2 Try not to intervene as he or she reads.
3 Encourage the child to initiate questions and air concerns.

Your purpose: to discover more about what the child is trying to do as he or she reads and to learn more about what is involved in the learning-to-read process.

Replay the tape with the text in front of you.

What did the child do?

1 Read word by word or in larger chunks of meaningful language?
2 Made informed guesses when encountering unfamiliar words/ phrases?
3 Read on when he or she came across a difficulty or looked to you for assistance?

4 Used initial letter sounds when faced with unfamiliar words?

5 Used expressive intonation to aid understanding?

6 Gave the impression that reading involved turning print into meaning?

What did you do?

1 At what points did you intervene?

2 Analyse what you said to the child. Were your utterances dependent on making sure that he or she got each word right? Or were they supportive of the notion that you were giving time and space for speculation, discussion, and shared enjoyment?

3 Have you a clearer picture of how you can further support this child's reading development?

Did the text enable the child to make sense of the activity?
Did the illustrations support and complement the text?

"Hello, monster," he said to the monster.

Suggestion

I have found it very helpful to make a list of the books that children *want* to read aloud to you. This list will provide a basis from which you can analyse what it is about a book that appeals; it will also act as a guide for future selection.

Examples

Here are two examples of children reading aloud, each with an explanatory commentary.

Example 1: Not Now Bernard

The story *Not Now Bernard* by David McKee was, in the first instance, read *to* Katy. Katy had been in school for one term; she was not yet five years old. As the story unfolded she continually asked questions, or passed comments, in her attempt to understand more fully the finer points and so relate this vicarious experience to what she already knew. The book's illustrations are delightful — complementary to, and supportive of, the text.

(It helps to have a copy of the book when you are studying the transcript.)

Actual text of Not Now, Bernard	Katy's interpretation of the text with the teacher's comments and tentative proposals
p. 1 *"Hello, Dad," said Bernard.*	p. 1 *Hello, Dad . . Not now . . said Bernard.* Katy attempted to recall the text and 'read' two pages in one! At this stage I intervened and asked her to show me where the story began. This was to see how far she was able to match the language in her head with the language on the page.
p. 2 *"Not now, Bernard," said his father.*	p. 2 *Not now, Bernard said his dad.* Interesting to note how she favoured the word 'dad' in preference to 'father'. The important factor here was that she was making an appropriate substitution based on her own social experiences: this alternative word does not alter the sense of the story.

p. 3 *"Hello, Mum," said Bernard.*

p. 3 *Hello, Mum said Bernard.*

p. 4 *"Not now, Bernard," said his mother.*

p. 4 *Not now, Bernard, said his mum.*
Used 'mum' instead of 'mother'.

p. 5 *"There's a monster in the garden and it's going to eat me," said Bernard.*

p. 5 *There's a monster in the garden and it's going to eat me, said Bernard.*
The pattern of language changed here and in order to support Katy and keep the story flowing, the first three words were read to her.

p. 6 *"Not now, Bernard," said his mother.*

p. 6 *Not now, Bernard, said his mother.*

p. 7 *Bernard went into the garden.*

p. 7 *Bernard went into the garden.*

p. 8 *"Hello monster," he said to the monster.*

p. 8 *Hello monster, said the . . . said the . . . Bernard.*
Katy became a little confused here. She wanted to get it right and yet the text did not conform to her expectations. Note that her primary concern was to make the text make sense.

p. 9 *The monster ate Bernard up, every bit.*

p. 9 *The monster ate Bernard up . . .*
Did it matter that she left out the last two words?

p.10 *Then the monster went indoors.*

p.10 *. . . He went indoors.*
Here, she predicted accurately but left out the link word.

p.11 *"ROAR," went the monster behind Bernard's mother.*

p.11 *ROAR, went the monster.*
The phrase, 'behind Bernard's mother' got in the way of her reading on so she left it out!

p.12 *"Not now, Bernard," said Bernard's mother.*

p.12 *Not now, Bernard, said his mother.*
Did she understand that the 'monster' was Bernard? Her interpretation would indicate that she did.

p.13 *The monster bit Bernard's father.*

p.13 *The monster bit his dad.*
Here again she presumed that the 'monster' was Bernard.

p.14 *"Not now, Bernard," said Bernard's father.*

p.14 *No, not now, Bernard, said his father.*
She changed the wording but not the meaning.

p.15 *"Your dinner's ready," said Bernard's mother.*

p.15 *Your supper's ready, said his mother.*

p.16 *She put the dinner in front of the television.*

p.16 *She put the lunch in front of the television.*
She used 'her' words for meal times. Did it matter?

p.17 *The monster ate the dinner.*

p.17 *The monster ate it all up.*
Here Katy's belief comes across that it is more socially acceptable to eat what is put in front of you.

p.18 *Then it watched the television.*

p.18 *Then it watched the television.*

p.19 *Then it read one of Bernard's comics.*

p.19 *Then it looked at one of Bernard's comics.*
Katy has already an understanding of the various ways in which you approach different kinds of texts. You *look* at comics, not *read* them!

p.20 *And broke one of his toys.*

p.20 *Then it broke one of his toys.*
She followed the language patterns of the previous two sentences.

p.21 *"Go to bed. I've taken up your milk," called Bernard's mother.*	p.21 *(Isn't he naughty?) Bernard it's time to go to bed.* She was concerned that the monster had, in her view, exhibited anti-social behaviour.
p.22 *The monster went upstairs.*	p.22 *So the monster went upstairs.* The word 'so' linked well with her interpretation of the text on the previous page.
p.23 *"But I'm a monster," said the monster.*	p.23 *I'm a monster.* This sentence was articulated with great stress on the 'I'm'.
p.24 *"Not now, Bernard," said his mother.*	p.24 *Not now, Bernard, said his mother.*

Katy has shared many books and stories with her parents at home. She came to school expecting to be able to learn to read. She already knows a great deal about stories and about written language. She is not over-concerned about getting every word right.

If you read her version of the text you will notice that she has a very clear understanding of the author's intent. As Margaret Meek has said in *Learning to Read*: 'We have to believe that if the young reader expects to take in hand the task of turning the print into meaning, getting the words exactly right will follow.' (p. 51)

Example 2: Kathy and Mark Book 5

Alistair was in the Top Infant class. He chose to read a book from the *Kathy and Mark* reading scheme (M. O'Donnell and R. Munro, Nisbet). He was familiar with the text and decided to read from the beginning of page 32. Alistair was always very apprehensive when asked to read aloud as he was convinced that he would not be able to perform well. But nobody can doubt his ability to learn; he has learnt so much from his teachers about one aspect of print and he adheres to this unfailingly.

What do you think was his chief reading strategy and did it help or hinder his understanding of the reading process?

Actual text of **Kathy and Mark**	Alistair's interpretation of the text
l. 1 Mark went into the house.	l. 1 Mark . . . Mark was in-t-to the house.
l. 2 Soon he came back.	l. 2 S . . Ser . . Ser . . . o . . . o . . . n. Some he c . . c . . c . . a . . m . . e . . came out. Soon he came out.
l. 3 "I have a surprise for you, Kathy," he said.	l. 3 It have . . . h . . h . . a . . v . . e . . . have . . . It have a s . . u . . r . . p . . s . . u . . r . . p . . r . . i . . s . . e . . suraya . . s . . s . . u . . r . . p . . sur, suraya . . . (I interrupt) a surprise for you, Kathy.
l. 4 "It is something little." "It is something green."	l. 4 He showed it to . . . it is good . . . it is something green. It is . . . something g . . g . . It is something little and it is something green.
l. 5 "You will like it."	l. 5 You with like it.
l. 6 "Do you want to see it?"	l. 6 D . . . Do you want it so see it? Do you want to see it?
l. 7 "Yes please," said Kathy.	l. 7 You p . . play . . . You . . . Yes please, said Kathy.
l. 8 "What is it? Show me."	l. 8 What is it? Said . . s . . os . . h . . o . . so . . m . . my . . me . . so me . . .

Alistair took an inordinate amount of time to read this passage. It was painful for him and painful for me. However, it was important not to intervene too frequently in order that there was opportunity to identify his strengths.

If you look at the transcript you will notice that Alistair could, in the final analysis, read the text for himself, but he felt bound to rely on his chief strategy (phonic analysis and synthesis). He does inadvertently try, on many occasions to make sense of the text — although the text is not supportive of this strategy — but this feeling that he must not rely on his own intuitions pervades his whole approach to the task.

Alistair's main strength is to put into action what he has been taught and he does this with commendable dedication and persistence.

Discussion points

Might Alistair benefit from a less prescriptive approach?
How could you help him build his own set of learning strategies?
Would it help if he were read to regularly? Why?
Which books would you make available to him?
In what other ways could you help him?

Children who do not succeed in learning to read in the primary school are those who come to believe that they are incapable of learning. This is the myth that we need to dispel.

Reading and our multi-cultural society
Sandra Smidt

Who is this chapter for?

Multi-cultural education has, in recent years, become something of a bandwagon. It has been aimed mainly at inner-city children – children from the West Indies, Africa, Asia, China, Greece, Turkey, Cyprus and many other countries. It has been felt that the needs of these children are special, different in some way from those of children in all-white English schools. In some respects this is, of course, true. The problems of learning English as a second language are particular to some of these children. But, in a broader sense, the deeper aim of multi-cultural education – that of eradicating ignorance, prejudice and racism – applies to all schools in this country.

All our children will grow up in a multi-cultural, multi-lingual society. In most classes in most schools the children are from varied backgrounds and experiences. In most classes there are children who are in some way systematically disadvantaged by our education system – girls, working class children, children who speak in dialect, black children, Irish children, children who have no English. For all these children and for their less disadvantaged peers it is essential to provide materials and opportunities which allow them to recognize and confront stereotypes, to become and remain critical and to acquire the knowledge and understanding of other languages and cultures which will move them away from our traditional ethnocentric perspective.

So, even if you teach in an all-white school in deepest Devon, this chapter is for you!

Meaning and the multi-cultural classroom

This is a personal anecdote – but one with meaning!

Some time ago, while on holiday in Italy, I went to a concert at which an American singer was performing. I bought a programme and during the interval tried to read the programme notes about the singer. The notes were in Italian and I know no Italian. Decoding was no

Some definitions

Certain words, like 'multi-cultural' and 'racism' are freely used in current educational jargon; indeed they are often misused, so it is necessary, at the start, to define our terms.

Race: a group of people connected by common descent. Biologically it means a variety within a species. Thus 'the English' are not a race. Physical characteristics which probably evolved as a result of environmental conditions are the factors which split the species (man) into 'races'.

Prejudice: an opinion made about people or things without adequate knowledge. From *pre* (before) and *judicium* (judge). A pre-judgement. It can be either positive or negative.

Racial prejudice: a hostile attitude to a group on the basis of 'observed' differences. This prejudice is, by definition, irrational and need not be expressed openly. It is usually based on mistaken ideas about race.

Racial discrimination: when racial prejudice takes an active, overt form. In this way groups may be denied access to things like jobs and housing.

Ethnic group: a group related by common descent and often shared values and beliefs, defined by its members as a group.

Multi-ethnic: containing many ethnic groups.

Culture: The 'intellectual' expression of a group of people; hence the language, literature, music, art, customs, science of a group of people.

Multi-cultural: containing many cultures.

Stereotype: a way of describing people which over-simplifies, over-generalizes and shows all individuals in a group as having the same characteristics. For example, all Jews are greedy; all the Irish are stupid. It is dangerous because it becomes a way of thinking and helps us to cling to our prejudices.

Ethno-centrism: one cultural heritage is regarded as superior to others. The beliefs, values and thinking of the 'superior' group are regarded as 'normal'. Anything else is called abnormal, bad, sick, deviant. For example, it is ethno-centric to say that the British brought civilization to India, the French brought it to Vietnam.

Racism: a mixture of prejudice, discrimination, stereotyping and ethno-centrism backed up by institutional power. It is used to the advantage of one 'racial' group and the disadvantage of another. The fact that one group has power is crucial. It is one form of oppression. Sexism is another.

problem. I could make the sounds of the language and with only a few errors would have been able to 'read aloud' the whole piece. Understanding was something quite different. Yet I found that I could make sense of most of the article and then tried to work out how I was able to make sense of a language that I did not know.

The first thing I observed was that I had certain expectations of what the piece would be about. From reading other programme notes I expected the account to be biographical – to tell me about the singer's career and achievements to date. The second thing I was able to do was to recognize certain words in the text. These tended to be English words or names like 'New York' or 'Boston'. Finally, I was able to guess at the meanings of certain words either because they were similar in form to English or French words, or because, by filling in gaps, I eliminated certain possibilities.

This experience was an important one for me because it put me in the position that many of our children are in when they are faced with an unfamiliar text or a text in an unknown language. It also clarified for me the difference between saying the words aloud and knowing what they mean.

Of course, I came to the task as a reader. I already knew that print conveys meaning and I had developed certain reading skills, like scanning. Nonetheless, the task was new to me. One of the reasons I was able to understand most of the text was that I was interested in it. Another was that I had had some experience of similar texts in English. Yet another was that it became a challenge and a game to be able to work out the meaning from the few clues I had. I certainly understood more of the Italian text that I was interested in than I did of an article I tried recently, in English, about corporations and high finance!

What are the implications of this for the multi-cultural, multi-lingual classroom?

---

1 Texts must be highly predictable.
2 Children are more likely to succeed with texts that are relevant and interesting to them.
3 Texts need to offer an adequate number of clues.
4 Experience of other similar texts will give children an advantage.
5 If the task is fun and challenging and there is no sense of failure, children will have the confidence to try.

Less directly, but equally important

6 Children are more likely to want to read things that offer them positive images of themselves and of their world and values.
7 Children need a varied diet of books, and this applies to the language of texts as well as to the range of texts. So classrooms need books in languages other than English, just as they need story books, fables, biographies, information books and dictionaries.

Where to start

The first things to look at in your classroom or school are the books your children read. Having accepted that children 'read by reading', then *what* they read matters.

Many books written for young children are about white middle class children in which boys are the active participants and girls their passive admirers and helpers. Picture books for younger children often contain the same stereotypes. Print and pictures are powerful. We tend to believe what we see in books. The influence exerted over us by print is acute and often subtle. For this reason it is important to look carefully at your books and at the images and messages they put across. If you find books which are offensive, I believe you ought to throw them out. There will be sufficient negative images remaining on television, in newspapers and comics which children can learn to recognize and be critical of.

Take any ten of your reading books. Inspect them in the light of this panel. How many offend you? Can you define why in each case? Remember that stereotypes are often subtle and hard to detect – their effect is always damaging. Remember too that both print and pictures convey meaning.

Mothers

Do they wear an apron, stay at home, cuddle the baby, cook, sew, knit, do the shopping, push the pram, smile a lot?

Is there any evidence of the reality of working mothers, wearing jeans, being tired, driving the car, mending a fuse?

Nurses

Invariably female, do they smooth down beds, mop fevered brows, take temperatures?

How much account is taken of male nurses and of the difficult and often technical nature of a nurse's work? Look, too, at the way in which other jobs are portrayed . . . doctors, bus drivers, teachers, postmen, etc.

Homes

Are they detached houses with lace curtains and a path leading down to the front gate? A garden? A garage?

How realistic is that for all the children who live in high rise flats, multi-tenant occupation, bed-sitters, hotels? Look, too, at the way in which schools and shops are shown. Do they reflect the reality of life for most of our children?

Granny

Is she white haired, bespectacled, hunched with wrinkly clothes?

How many of your children's grannies are really like this?

*Black children**

Are there any? If so, are they the key characters or just shown on the fringes as a token gesture. Are they drawn with exaggerated facial features or do they show a full range of facial characteristics shown in European children?

Families

Mum, Dad, boy, girl – the 'typical' nuclear family? Does boy always help Dad and have adventures? Is he strong and brave – maybe even occasionally naughty? Does the girl help Mum with the domestic tasks? Is she pretty, passive and neat? And do they all live in the sort of house mentioned above?

How real is this for the children of separated parents, children from large families, children in single parent families, adopted children?

* 'Black' in this context is used to refer to all non-white children.

Being positive

Having discarded all the books you and your children find offensive, you will now want to replace them with the increasing number of new books which show children of all racial types, girls, working class children, all playing important roles. But beware of tokenism . . . the one black child on the fringe of the group, for example.

Here are some examples of new books which have good illustrations, thoughtful text and avoid showing people as stereotypes.

Babylon, by J. P. Walsh.
Alex and Roy: *Alex's Outing* by M. Dickinson.
Berron's Tooth and others by J. Solomon.
How We Live by A. Harper and C. Roche.
The Terraced House Series by P. Heaslip.
ILEA, *Reading Through Understanding*.
The Fancy Dress Party by G. Klein and S. Willby.
Dig Away Two-Hole Tim by J. Agard.

There are, of course, many more.

There are also a number of useful publications which review books and suggest those that are not offensive. I suggest you use these publications as a guide, but make sure that you look at the books yourself before ordering them. Some of the publications are:
Children's Book Bulletin from Children's Rights Workshop.
Resources for multicultural education, Klein (82), Schools' Council.
Wider Heritage, National Book League.
Dragon's Teeth: Bulletin of National Committee on Racism in Children's Books.

If you are choosing books go and look at your local bookshops, keep up to date and go to the book exhibitions that are held by publishers to promote their materials.

Dual-language texts

Part of our aim, as teachers, must be to equip children to cope with this education system. That implies helping all our children to become proficient in reading and writing English. It is increasingly apparent that the way to do this is to value what the children bring to school. This means valuing their culture and their language. There is a long tradition in this country that our language is the superior language and our culture the superior culture. This is one of our most damaging myths. There is no one 'superior' culture or language.

In all classrooms it would make sense to have some books with dual-language texts. This shows children that other languages can be written and read and that they have form and value. The best place to start is in the Nursery or Infant school. The following are useful publications.

L. Wilson, *City Kids* (4 packs of 6 books in English, plus Greek, Italian, Turkish and no-text).
Ezra Jack Keats' books.
P. Heaslip, The Terraced House Series (with stick-in translations).

Even if all the children in your class speak only English they need to have books around them in other languages so that they become aware that people do read in other languages. In multi-lingual classrooms the books you choose should, of course, be related to the languages spoken by your children. You will have to put some effort into finding suitable dual language books and, if all else fails, make your own!

One of the problems of buying non-English books is that unless one is able to read the particular language, it is impossible to assess the text. Is it racist? Imperialist? Sexist? Propaganda? Readable? Predictable? Interesting? Appropriate for the age and interests of your children?

A Hackney initiative

The children in a Hackney school were asked to choose their six favourite books from a selection limited according to the simplicity of the text and the space available on each page to add translations.

The texts were then translated into the main languages of the school – Bengali, Urdu, Gujerati, Turkish and Punjabi. The translations were carried out by the professional translation unit of the Inner London Education Authority. Each translation was then photocopied, cut up and pasted into the books alongside the English text.

For each book a tape recording of the story was made in both English and one of the other languages. Using these materials, children, wearing headphones, can share the books, follow the text and hear the story in English and several other languages.

"Can you make room for me?" said the calf.

"Yes, if you don't trample about."

کیا آپ میرے لئے بھی جگہ نکال سکتے ہیں پھٹرے نے کہا

ہاں اگر تم اتارو نہیں

This scheme involves a great deal of work and there are simpler ways of making your own dual language texts. Parents, brothers, sisters, secondary school pupils, community leaders and members of staff can be involved in translating existing books. Remember, it is important to translate not only from English into other languages, but also from other languages into English.

Making books

Children as authors

Some of the most popular and readable materials in schools are books written by the pupils. Children compose a story, perhaps on their own, perhaps with a friend. The story is then either written up and made into a book, or typed by child or adult — perhaps on a Jumbo typewriter. Such books, photocopied and illustrated, make excellent reading material and, of course, they can be translated. Parents and other members of the family, or local people, will help with translations and it is possible to build up a good selection of dual-language books in this way.

In one school, stories written by children were translated and produced for sale to local schools. A page from one of these books is shown below.

In this case the home language of the author was different from the language into which the book was translated.

Parents as authors

Just as children are interested in stories written by their peers, they are interested in stories written specifically for them by their parents. Parents often write about their own childhood, about their

Köyde annem, babam ve küçük kız-
kardeşimle beraber yaşadım.

I lived with my parents and younger
sister in the country.

Two pages from a book written by a parent for her child. The book was written at a workshop for parents at William Patten Infant School.

2

In the Zoo there are lots of different animals to see. This is a flamingo.

Daddy took us there in the car. We left it in the car park.

Two pages of a book written by children for other children. Produced by Princess May Junior School, London.

schooling or about their child's babyhood. Such books may be written in English, mother tongue or dialect. Children or parents can illustrate them and, again, they can be translated.

It is important not to be too concerned with accurate grammar or spelling. Children reading these texts for meaning will make sense of them.

Asking parents to become writers or translators needs to be handled sensitively. Some parents cannot write; many may be intimidated if the task seems too formal or forbidding. So, go carefully!

Comics

Comics are still read and loved by most children. They also seem to be universal – despite the fact that they are often riddled with sexism, propaganda and the most blatant of stereotyping! But the notion of a cheap publication using comic strip, jokes, cartoons and riddles is a useful one to borrow and adapt.

On pages 40 and 41 are some pages from a primary school comic. The teacher in this case was active in planning the first few editions, but the children soon took over and the comics, sold for 1p or 2p per copy, were very popular. People in the local community were asked to help with translations and adults and children both contributed to the comics.

Bookshops

Here is a list of London bookshops. If you are not in a large city these booksellers will be able to send you booklists and sometimes inspection copies.

General Bookshops

Centreprise
136 Kingsland High Street, London E8 2NS

Sisterwrite (Feminist bookshop)
190 Upper Street, London N1 1RQ

Ujamaa Centre
14 Brixton Road, London SW9 6BU

Afro-Caribbean Bookshops

Headstart Books and Crafts
25 West Green Road, London N15 5BX

Third World Bookshop
28 Sackville Street, London W1X 1DA

Indian Sub-Continent

Books from India
69 Great Russell Street, London WC1B 3BN

Soma Books
c/o The Commonwealth Institute
Kensington High Street, London W8

(continued on page 41)

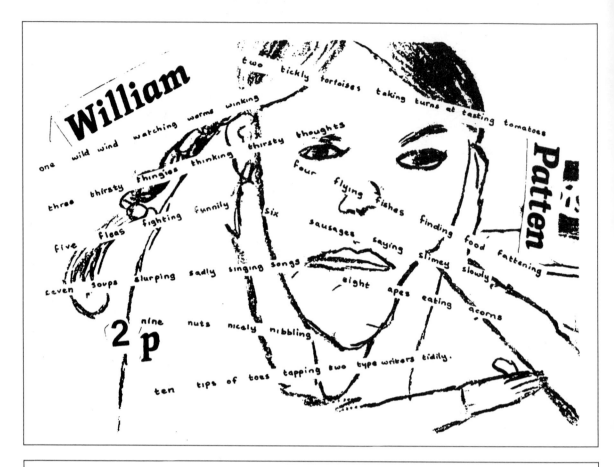

Pages from a comic ▲

Pages from a comic ▲

Arabic Books

Al Saqi Books
26 Westbourne Grove, London W2 5RH

Muslim Bookshop
233 Seven Sisters Road, London N4 2DA

Greek Books

Hellenic Book Service
122 Charing Cross Road, London WC2H 0JR

Turkish Books

Basaran Türk Kitabevi
117 Green Lanes, London N16 9DA

Japanese Books

O.C.S. Bookshop
67 Parkway, London NW1 7PP

Chinese Books

Guanghwa Bookshop
9 Newport Place, London WC2H 7JR

Farsi Books

Iran Book Centre
233 Old Brompton Road, London SW5 0EA

Polish Books

Orbis Books
66 Kenway Road, London SW5 0RD

Western European Languages

Grant and Cutler
11 Buckingham Street, London WC2N 6DF

A checklist

1 Is your book corner attractive and peaceful and does it reflect the experiences, languages and interests of your children?

2 Have you checked that the books in it do not reflect negative images or show people as stereotypes?

3 Do you change the books frequently?

4 Do you make use of your local library and try to persuade them to include a wider range of books?

5 Do you encourage the children to look after and value books?

6 Are your children allowed to take the books home? You will lose some, but many children don't have books at home, so it is a worthwhile risk to take.

7 Do you invite parents and people from the

community in to read with the children? Do you try to encourage parents to read in their own language? Do you make tape recordings of parents reading in their mother tongue?

8 Do you invite story tellers into school – particularly people able to read and tell stories from other cultures and in other languages?

9 Do you celebrate 'Book Week' in your school?

10 Do you ever write book reviews for your children or for your colleagues? Do the children ever review books for you and for each other?

11 Do you have a regular school bookshop? Does it sell dual language and mother tongue books?

12 Do you make use of children's writing, parents' writing and your own writing to make books, comics and newspapers for distribution to the class or school?

Multi-lingual classrooms

It is important for you, as teacher, to know what language or languages your children speak at home. You may be very surprised to find how many languages one child may speak and/or understand. You may also be surprised to discover that children can often read and write in several languages. Do you know whether or not the child speaks in dialect?

There is the danger of bilingual children being labelled as 'slow' and being referred for remedial help. Such children, already proficient in one or more languages, may need special help, but their abilities should not be underestimated. Similarly, certain children appear to be fluent in spoken English and it is easy to overlook the fact that English for them is still a second language.

One case study

Rezaur was a six-year-old Iranian boy, very boisterous and talkative. Yet he was not learning to read as quickly as one might have predicted from his obvious abilities. It later emerged that at home his parents spoke only Farsi and that he was so busy learning to speak and comprehend English that he was not yet interested in learning to read. Because of his apparent fluency the school had overlooked the fact that for him English was still a second language.

In many inner city schools there are now teachers who specialize in teaching English as a second language. Happily, the days when second language learners were consigned to remedial groups are past. These children should spend as much time as possible with their own class. Children learn most from their peers and in situations in which they are motivated to communicate. They also need to feel secure, willing to take chances and make mistakes. If the classroom is too noisy to allow them to concentrate on specific listening activities then they should be withdrawn to a quieter place only briefly. Any temporary withdrawal group should include fluent English speaking children in order to provide models.

In the classroom, second language learners can be supported in learning English by working collaboratively or in small groups (see box on page 43). There are a number of learning situations which are useful in helping children develop confidence in expressing complex thoughts in the new language.

In this situation the children helped each other and when they were stuck handed on to another child. So, no failure, a lot of fun and some hard work in constructing a meaningful text. It is important to note that in this group of six and seven year olds Amy and Michael were fluent English speakers and Shamin had only just started to speak English. Shamin and Ayten are good friends and support each other.

A listening corner is essential in a classroom. A quiet place where tape recorder, headphones and language master are set out together with books and tapes for children to listen to and share. A collection of English, mother tongue and dual language books and tapes should be built up. If a language master is used the sentences written on cards should sometimes be in English, sometimes in mother tongue and sometimes in dual-language.

Nursery rhymes and songs have long been used as a way of helping children become readers. Since it is difficult (if not impossible) to find mother tongue or dual-language editions of such rhymes these can be made by class teachers with the help of parents and older children. Books made of these songs and rhymes, plus accompanying tapes, should also be available to children in the listening corner.

Games, similarly, are an excellent opportunity for children to communicate, but be careful to select games which are open-ended and require children to do more than give one word answers. Try and avoid competitive games. 'What's in a Square?' is an excellent game in which children have to fit objects on cards into given categories and then explain why. You can make your own games based on children's interests.

Scholastic Publications and Arnold/Wheaton (*Story Chest*) produce a series of 'Big Books' which are useful with less confident children. The large book can be placed on a stand and the teacher or another child reads the story over and over again. During the reading the teacher can point to the text which is clearly visible to the group of children, sometimes asking 'What will happen next?' or 'And then what happens?'. The group of children will enjoy constructing the text and referring to the pictures.

Group activity

A group of children were each given a card with a noun on it and the whole group was given the ending of the story. The aim of the exercise was to make up a story including each of the nouns and to work towards the ending. The children were to help each other and the group was tape-recorded at work.

Transcript

Amy (English), Michael (Chinese), Ayten (Turkish), Shamin (Bengali).

The nouns were bag, flowers, house, bread. The ending was '. . . and the dragon went back to his cave and was never seen again.'

Amy:	I'll start. 'Once upon a time a girl lived in a house.'
Michael:	What about the dragon?
Amy:	What dragon?
Michael:	You have to have the dragon 'cos he's there . . . see . . . he's there . . . .
Ayten:	Yeah, he's at . . at . . . he's the ending.
Amy:	I know. 'Once upon a time the girl lived in a house near this dragon and then . . . and then . . .' it's your turn, Ayten.
Ayten:	Um . . . . um . . . 'she lived near this dragon, see, and he . . . he was fierce . . . .'
Michael:	What about the bag?
Ayten:	'. . . and one day she went to see her Granny and she had a bag . . .' your turn, Michael.
Michael:	'and she stopped to pick flowers.' Hey! This is like Red Riding Hood!
Others:	Yeah!
Michael:	'. . . and this dragon came up and he said "I'll eat you up" and she said . . .' your turn Shamin.
Shamin:	'She said . . . she said . . . she say . . . "I'll give you my bread" and . . . and . . .' you now, Ayten.
Ayten:	'The dragon said "Yum, yum, I love bread." And then he ran away.'
Amy:	Good, good. We got it. '. . . and the dragon ran away . . . went back to his cave and was never seen again.'

This can be extended to the group of children writing a similar big book for themselves, making up the text collaboratively. The teacher, in this situation, is the scribe.

Dialect speakers

Reading, says Kenneth Goodman, is a 'psycholinguistic guessing game' where each unknown word is worked out not letter by letter, but from its context. Just as smaller children learning to talk use all available clues, so does the reader. All clues – grammatical, semantic and visual, are used to narrow down the possibilities.

We know that the mistakes children make when reading aloud are a valuable indication of the way in which they are reading and of what can be done to help them. A child may completely alter the meaning, or may preserve the meaning but replace an unfamiliar word with a more familiar one. Or, again, a child may get the meaning and the word right but may alter the grammar according to the rules of his or her own dialect. For example, a West Indian child may read 'boys' as 'boy' or 'looked' as 'look'. These errors actually indicate that the child has understood the text and is using his or her linguistic competence to recreate meaning.

So miscue analysis is important when hearing dialect speakers read. There are dangers here in the way in which we, as teachers, view and handle such miscues. If we say things like 'Look more closely at the end of the words' we may be conveying a double meaning to the child. The notion that the child's English is unacceptable, implicit in the instruction to pay particular attention to individual words, may divert him or her from his or her search for meaning.

Another implication of considering dialect is the importance of selecting reading materials for children which increase their chances of being right by using the sort of language which children themselves use. Many reading schemes are notorious for not doing this. Even dialogue – what little there is – is couched in formal language. For example, 'Would you like a drink?' rather than the more common form 'Do you want a drink?'. Of course one wants to retain book language with all its fluency and formality, but it is also important to include books that use more informal speech.

A third implication of considering dialect is the context in which the child reads. Reading is often seen as a testing situation, if not by the teacher, then often by the child. It is a situation, however warm and friendly, where the child's performance is being evaluated. It is important, then, to provide situations in which children read with and to each other.

Several such situations have already been outlined (using Big Books, reading together with headphones).

The Centre for Urban Educational Studies has published a set of books designed for just such 'paired' reading called *Reading Through Understanding*. Each book is designed to be read by a fluent and a less fluent reader. Some of the books are accompanied by cards which can be used to make up the story. All the books are accompanied by tapes. Simple plays for the children to read in a group can also be useful, but take care that the language used is not too old-fashioned and stilted.

Group activity

Cloze procedure is carried out as a group activity where the aim is for the children to argue and agree on the missing words in a text. In order to do this they have to persuade each other that their choice makes the most sense.

Transcript

Corin (English), Hussain (Turkish), Sharon (West Indian), Sandra (Greek).

Corin:	Right, I'm in charge.
Sharon:	No you not. Miss say....
Corin:	O.K. I'll read it. 'One day there was a little blank.'
Hussain:	That's girl.
Corin:	O.K.... 'girl'. Now I'll read it. 'One day there was a little girl.' Is that it?
Sandra:	Yes.
Sharon:	Yes.
Corin:	Let's go on. 'His name was Ali.'... Hey!...
Sharon:	Come on, Corin. Give we... us give us a chance. I'll read it now. 'One day....'
Hussain:	Don't go back. We've done that one.
Corin:	But....
Sharon:	What's the next one, then?
Corin:	No! We have to go back 'cos there's a 'his' and we said 'girl'.
Sharon:	'One day there was a little girl. His name was Ali.'
Sandra:	'HIS name'... no... it... if... if it's a girl it's 'her name'.
Sharon:	'One day there was a little girl. Her name was Ali.'
Hussain:	NO! NO! Ali... that's a boy....
Corin:	I know. I've got it. It's not girl it's boy.

The actual word is almost irrelevant in this case. What matters is the discussion, the argument and the search for meaning. The problem encountered in this example was one of gender – a fairly common problem for second language learners.

Mother tongue . . . Why bother?

The question of mother tongue teaching is one which causes passionate debate. There are those who believe that, by concentrating on the child's home language, the language needed for success in this country is being ignored. There are others who argue hotly that it is essential for the learning of English that the child's language and culture be respected and kept alive.

The question is quite simple really. Children who come to school speaking another language are fortunate. They are as fortunate as those coming to school as gifted musicians, mathematicians and footballers. Schools don't hesitate to encourage such skills and it seems imperative that other languages are regarded as highly as the more traditionally accepted academic skills. The child's mother tongue has been taught by his or her parents and often it is the only means of communication between child and parent. Children who live in England, go to school in England, watch TV in England, will learn English because they need to and they want to. They are more likely to succeed in the formal skills of reading and writing in English if the school accepts that they can write in another language and regards their bilingualism as a valued asset.

Of course there are logistical problems. If you have seventeen different languages in your school how can they all be taught, when and by whom? One of the answers lies with the staffing of schools. Schools where there is a high concentration of particular language groups should demand the services of teachers speaking these languages. When schools are appointing ancillary staff this is an issue that should be borne in mind.

In the classroom, much of what has been said in this chapter will help children keep their home languages alive. You will need to provide mother tongue books, ask parents and others to help with translations and, most of all, create an environment in which it is apparent that you regard bilingualism as an asset and not as a problem.

Teachers have to be aware of the context and philosophy underlying their multi-cultural teaching. In order to come to terms with the problems faced by our children, teachers have to be more committed to anti-racist teaching. This is not about direct political indoctrination; rather, it is about being honest with children, about recognizing the rights of children and, most importantly, the inherent racism which exists in some parts of our society.

You can systematically throw out all offensive books, make dual language books, encourage children to write in Urdu and be sensitive when listening to dialect children read. But unless you have two main objectives in mind you might as well not bother. You have to be vigilant in maintaining an environment in which minority children − particularly black children − are not systematically disprivileged. Also you have to ensure that the environment you create, embodying racial and cultural diversity, actively encourages the groups within the class to understand each other and to care for each other. This implies that you, as a teacher, are prepared to face the issues that confront most of our children − those of racism, prejudice and ignorance − and to consider these as much part of the core curriculum as the more hallowed topics of sets, phonics and pets.

Some questions

1 Do you know what language(s) the children in your class speak/write/read?

2 Do you ensure that second language learners spend most of their time in the classroom and not in a withdrawal group?

3 Do you have a place in your room where children can listen to tapes and use a language master? Do you check the books and tapes. Do they reflect the languages, interests, cultures of your children?

4 Do children always read to a teacher? Is there any collaborative reading/paired reading/silent reading?

5 How do you make sure that all children in the class understand what is required of them? Particularly children whose first language is not English.

6 What opportunities are there in your class for children to write in their home language?

7 Do the pictures, posters, etc., in your class reflect only one culture or many? Do they reflect the cultures of the children in your class? Do they reflect these cultures in a positive light?

8 Look carefully at the games you play with children: how open-ended are they?

9 What scope is there in your room for children to work collaboratively when reading/writing/talking?

10 How do you think it feels to be a child in your class?

A last word

In primary schools all over Britain children make pappadoms, dance to Greek music, play African drums. However, a 'tokenist' approach to 'multi-cultural education' can divorce 'culture' from the child's real way of living. It does not start from where the children are, and some members of the immigrant communities may see it as a subtle means of social control.

Further reading

Edwards, A. D. E., *Language in Culture and Class: the Sociology of Language and Education*, Heinemann Educational Books, 1976.

Kuya, D., 'Schoolbooks attacked for warped outlook on race', *The Guardian*, 17 April 1971.

Milner, D., *Children and Race*, Penguin, 1975.
        Children and Race; ten years on, Ward Lock Educational, 1983.

Smith, F., *Understanding Reading: a psycholinguistic analysis of reading and learning to read*, Holt, Rinehart and Winston, 1979.

Stones, M., *The Education of the Black Child in Britain: the Myth of Multi-Racial Education*, Fontana, 1981.

Reading and learning
Shirley Paice

A shop near me advertises 'Real Sausages'. There are many devotees of 'real ale' and 'organic honey' (whatever that may be!), and cafés serve 'Mother's original apple pie'. We are beginning to revolt against the artificial and the mass-produced.

In the same way, many children nowadays are learning to read with 'real' books, works of literary and artistic merit, rather than with tedious reading schemes. We hope that this will lead them to a lifelong love affair with the world of fiction.

We cannot, however, exist on an exclusive diet of literature. Many times each day adults resort to works of reference – telephone directories, bus timetables, instructions and diagrams, dictionaries – and to specialist books on an amazing variety of subjects from campanology to computers. We need to know

something. Knowing how to find the answers to our questions is enabling power. Often it is as important to be able to make sense of a tax form, to find out when our favourite programme is on, or to spell a word correctly for a job application, as it is to commune with the writer of a great novel.

Primary age children need guidance in reading reference books of all kinds from the time they first pick up such a book of their own accord. They need help to recognize and respond to the non-fiction voice, to use the book, to be master of it. And just as young children will more effectively learn to enjoy fiction by reading real books, so they need good, honest information books of many different kinds and to be shown the special ways we use them.

In some of our schools the provision of non-fiction

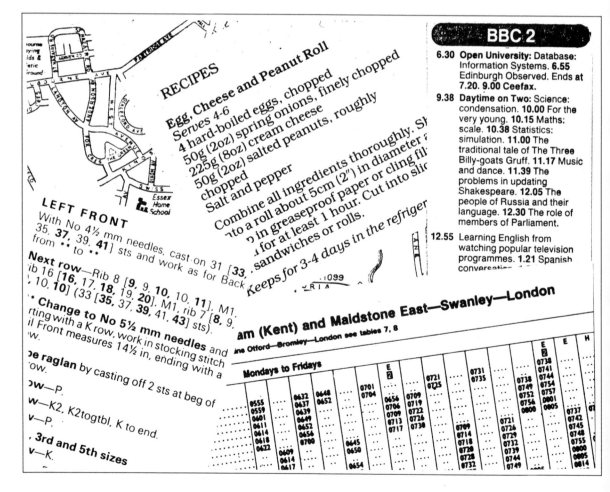

seems to be judged by quantity rather than quality. Bad books are not just useless; they are harmful. We should not send to the secondary school children who are unwilling and unable to use information books. One thing is certain, at eleven they will be presented with far more non-fiction than fiction, and they really need to know their way around it.

'If all else fails, read the instructions'

There are certainly plenty of adults who have great difficulty in using everyday resources such as telephone directories or road maps.

If we help the children in our classes to become confident and proficient in the use of various sources of 'real' information they will gain a useful skill for life.

It is preferable, of course, that this work is not done in the form of isolated exercises. If possible there should be a definite reason for the enquiry. Perhaps the class wishes to contact an outside expert to help with a topic. Maybe they are going on a train journey.

As soon as children can read a little we should be showing them how to use simple directories such as British Telecom's Yellow Pages.

If it is well designed, the diagram giving instructions for making a working model, perhaps for science work, can be a great incentive to a young reader (see page 49).

Ask your children

1 Which of these do you see your parents using?
2 Which could you use without help?

Dictionary

Railway or bus timetable

Map or road atlas

Knitting pattern

Concert programme

Radio/TV Times

Telephone directory

Tax form, or similar

Catalogue

Why non-fiction?

When we talk of non-fiction for young readers we generally think of dictionaries, sets of encyclopedias, and 'topic' books of various kinds. Most schools and many classrooms contain some or all of these which we expect the children to use for their work.

It would be a good thing first to ask why we use information books at all with young children. Ideally they will learn from first-hand experience and from direct contact with experts and enthusiasts. (Have you ever tried to learn basketry from a book?) They will make their own environmental studies and records.

Of course, the time will come when the expert is not available. We are a bit short of ancient Egyptians in school, or even Egyptologists. Books are a permanent, portable, manageable resource. Additionally, the use of non-fiction books will promote the growth of certain specific reading skills.

Early readers

For early readers, the non-fiction book has, I believe, two main uses.

1   The consolidation of known facts

These facts will be a blend of what the child already knows, and perhaps what we or some educational broadcast have told him or her.

2   The introduction to the genre of non-fiction

The young child's first literary experience is that of the story. Children tell themselves stories of what they experience as soon as they begin to understand words, but they need to learn exactly what an information book is.

Fluent readers

As soon as children become fluent readers, other skills in the use of information books can be added.

3   Ordering and organizing information

The arrangement of various facts into a logical order must take place if we are to retain them and make use of them in drawing conclusions. It is essential that the books we choose from for our children will not hinder this process.

4   Learning new information of their own choice

When children seek books to extend their own knowledge we know that they are well on the way to the mature reading of non-fiction.

Topics

Whether or not we aim to teach regularly through topics, there will come a time in every classroom when we arrange a display on a particular subject. Perhaps the class is going to visit a nearby wood or, in our case, the Otter Trust in Suffolk. Maybe they saw a television programme about railways or bread making. A display with pictures, objects, and books is a familiar sight.

A display of different types of books.

I try to make available a wide range of books, both fiction and non-fiction, advanced and simple. The County Library Service, local teachers' centres, and local advisers can all be very helpful. *Child Education* and *Junior Education* publish useful project book lists.

The topic books in the illustration above include all grades of resource, from an adult reference book to a home-made caption book. The pictures in many of these topic books are very attractive, but problems often arise when we try to read them aloud. In an attempt to simplify, many writers use a terse unimaginative style which has a very discouraging effect on teacher and listener. It may be argued that non-fiction is not intended to be read aloud, but beginning readers seldom seem to read silently. (That may be our fault, not theirs!)

When their interest is aroused children will make tremendous efforts to read non-fiction books and can succeed in understanding writing we would consider quite beyond them, but more often their efforts are unrewarded. I believe that in presenting children with text that is boring or incomprehensible to them we are doing them a great disservice. In fact we are laying the foundations for poor use of reference books later on.

Start where the children are

Many writers of juvenile non-fiction seem unable to put themselves 'where the children are'. Children are not little blank slates waiting to be written on: they have their own experiences and ideas on many subjects. When writing about ladybirds, for example, it is not necessary to tell a six-year-old that ladybirds are generally red and black; it *is* necessary to say that they are a type of beetle. It is also necessary to answer the kind of questions that children actually ask, for example, 'Are the seven-spot ladybirds older than the two-spot?' and 'Do they bite?'

It is not possible for beginning readers to do very much independent reading with topic books. In their earliest stages they will look at the pictures and attempt to read the captions. But even at this point children can learn how to be critical readers. Once they grasp the essential fact that just because something is in print it is not necessarily infallible, it is remarkable what quite young children notice. I have had seven-year-olds commenting on conflicting information about otter cubs. At what age do they leave the holt? Do their parents teach them to swim or not? There was no consensus about this in our books!

Learning how to use non-fiction

Sooner or later someone working on a topic will ask for help. This is the teacher's opportunity to show him or her how to use information books. Then the use of a contents list and index can be demonstrated and also the act of skimming down a page quickly. Further, if working alongside a mature seven- or eight-year-old, the teacher can point out the bibliography and explain that the topic book only touches on the beginnings of the subject. The child must not get the impression that any book is the last word on the subject.

> **Try this**
>
> Give about twenty of your books — fiction and non-fiction mixed — to a pair of your children and ask them to sort them out. Tape their conversation. You may find out that they have only a very hazy idea of what constitutes non-fiction.

The non-fiction voice

Able children will soon begin to distinguish between fiction and non-fiction books. I believe it is important for us to include in book corners genuine information books as well as the *Greeny was a Frog* type of story. (No-one would deny that real fiction can be genuinely informative. *Stig of the Dump* by Clive King can tell us a lot about cavemen while remaining primarily a very good story.)

The information book not only introduces young children to a collection of facts but to a way of organizing and setting down those facts. Non-fiction has a distinctive voice and style; even titles can be confusing. I have a book about bees which shows a mass of them on the comb. The title is *The Bee*. A child asked me, 'Which one?' This use of the singular takes some time to understand. At first one has to explain that 'the tadpole' means all tadpoles and 'early man' means men, women, and children. All these are important lessons.

The fact that children may have problems does not mean that we should not work with non-fiction as well as fiction. Children work very well together helping each other find and record interesting information.

In addition to this collaboration in learning, children also need direct teaching, not usually as a class, but individually or in small groups.

The transcriptions on page 50 reflect some of the learning that takes place in my class of six- and seven-year-olds.

▲
Becoming a critical reader
Sara, 'What does your book say about brontosauruses, Kevin?'

Lucy aged six can already understand and use many of the conventions of diagrams. She has numbered her drawings. Arrows show which items are put into the bucket.

▼

Andrew and Neill are using pictures alone and ignoring the text.

A: I've found out that the web comes out of the spider's tail here.

T: See if you can find out if the mother or father spider makes the web, or if they both can.

T: What kind of duck is that?

N: Don't know.

T: Look, it's written underneath. A shoveller duck.

Ben and John are comparing information given with what they already know.

B: *(reading)* 'Otters steer with their tails.' *(laughing)* I don't usually do that. I change my body round.

J: *(reading)* 'Bats eat insects that come out at night.' And some types bite people too, don't they?

Laura is learning how to generalize.

T: How would you find out about otters?

L: *(looking at index)* Um, water animals?

Deborah is beginning to scan a page.

D: The cobra has a hood.

T: Why? To keep it dry?

D: No. I'll have a look. *(She slides her finger up and down the text)* Yes, it's for 'threatening'.

Arranging a book corner

I assume that you have already provided a quiet area where your children are encouraged to read and enjoy books. Often all kinds of books are gathered at random on the racks and shelves. Perhaps you prefer children to read fiction and non-fiction as they find it.

In my classroom I separate the books as a first step towards learning library skills. I call the fiction 'story books' and the non-fiction 'information' or 'finding out' books. Poetry, prayer books and Bible stories are included with the fiction. Near the information books, but accessible from outside the quiet area, is a table containing various types of word books and dictionaries.

The non-fiction is not arranged in categories at all, neither according to subject nor difficulty. The children are six and seven, and I am not convinced that any sort of colour coding is appropriate.

These are some of the things I do in my classroom:

1 I make the book corner comfortable and inviting.

2 I introduce all new books enthusiastically to the class.

3 I display at least some books with their covers facing outwards.

4 I have times for silent reading and join in myself.

5 I let children help keep books tidy.

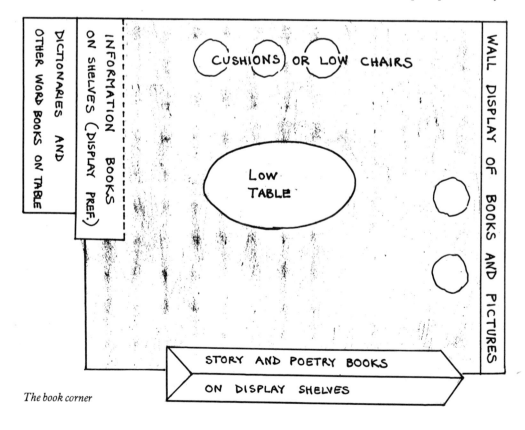

The book corner

These are some of the things I don't do

1 I don't have rows and rows of just one series of books.

2 I don't keep out-of-date or tatty books.

3 I don't forget to read non-fiction as well as fiction to the children.

4 I don't treat reading as something to do when the children have finished their work or 'while I mark the register'.

Types of non-fiction books in primary schools

What use do you make of any or all of these types of non-fiction in your school?

Dictionaries
1 *Picture word books* Generally arranged in themes.
2 *Simple alphabetical*

Encyclopedias
1 *One-volume alphabetical* Often over-simplified, with eccentric choice of items.
2 *Multi-volume 'children's encyclopedias'*
(a) Alphabetical – sometimes poor cross-referencing.
(b) Subject based – very difficult to track down information.

Text books
Often History or Geography. One chapter for each period or country. Can be inaccurate in fact or dated in emphasis.

Topic books
1 *Part of an extensive series.* Compiled by a committee for world market. Bland, flat style, unreliable.
2 *Single books, by a committed enthusiast.* Often harder reading but more rewarding.

Original source material
This could include:
1 *Old school record books.*
2 *Information collected by pupils from their families and other local people.*
3 *Information collected by pupils' personal observation.*

Working with older primary children

Children of nine and ten are often encouraged to write stories for the younger children to read. Having to write for an audience like this helps them to think about their work in a special way.

I asked my colleague Peter Brierley to help me find out how much the oldest children in the primary school really understood about information books, and how to choose the right one and use it. We decided that it would be a good exercise to ask the children to explain their strategies clearly and simply for younger children. Not only was the method quite successful for our needs, but it proved an effective way to teach the children how to use the reference library. They wrote out instructions for themselves and each other, tested them out and then re-wrote and re-tested. Some produced very clear directions indeed.

It was obvious that some children were better than others at asking themselves the right questions. David wanted to find out about swimming. He suggested that he might find information by looking at associated subjects: 'If you cannot find what you want, these are some words you might look at – sports, hobbies, water sport, achievements, famous people, and water safety.'

I doubt whether many experienced writers could have produced a better explanation than Leila, aged 10.

How to find information in a library

If you're looking for a book about, say, Zebras you must first think about what sort of book you want, in this case it would be in a book of animals. If your library has sections you should look for the section called Nature. When you have found it you must look for the number that is called Animals then find a book in that section with that number and look in the index under Z and if the book has not got an index look in the contents, read the page number it says and turn to it and it should be about Zebras.

If the book has neither index nor contents scanning the page for sub-titles or pictures about or of Zebras may help you to find out about them as there might well be writing near them about Zebras.

However, these children cannot manage entirely on their own. Let Emma have the last word.

If the book has not got an index look for the contents and go to the page and then read through, if you cannot find it ask for HELP.

Locating information in the library.

Children making their own information books

When children are making careful observations and recording them, they are able to make their own information books.

Katie can understand and use the conventions of her medium. The drawings which she originally made on three separate occasions have been copied by her onto one diagram. She is less certain about text. The three statements may or may not be in the best order.

Not until we have tried to draw a map which can be followed, or a diagram which can be used, do we realize that to organize information in this way requires a great deal of thought. Children need practice in making maps and all sorts of diagrams. The planning, drafting, rejecting and re-drafting are all part of a subtle learning process even for entertaining work like this.

Katie's information on beans.

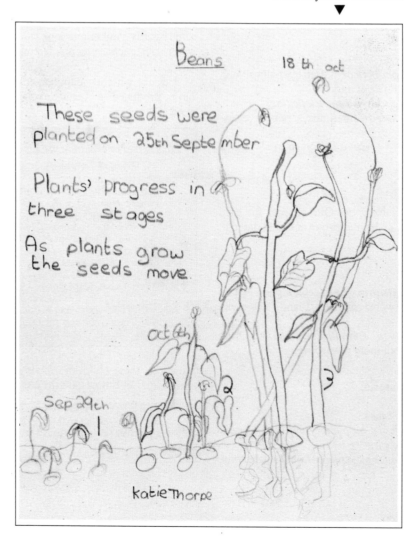

Practical work

Illustrated opposite is a page from a most successful practical information book by Isao Honda called *Origami*. The folded cup on the table is a genuine piece of origami glued onto the page. Generations of enthusiastic children have used this book to produce birds, boxes, and many other quite intricate objects.

How to choose information books for young readers

Teachers are busy people, but time taken to choose really valuable information books for our school is well used. If we succumb to the fatal lure of the series we may end up with many useless books. First and foremost we should read the books we intend to buy, preferably out loud. It is remarkable how many books in schools are chosen from publishers' 'blurbs' and are then read by neither teacher nor pupil.

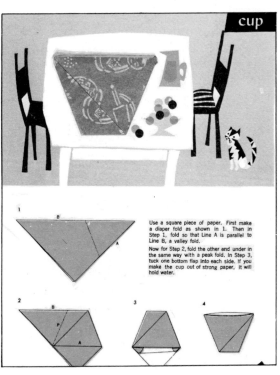

Learning to use co-ordinates on a large-scale local ordnance survey map which includes the school and the roads where the children live.

These are some of the main criteria I use when choosing non-fiction

1   Attractive cover

The children will not even open the book if the front cover is unappealing.

2   Clear layout

Children should not be overwhelmed by close text or words printed over a strongly-coloured background. They must be able to see which writing belongs to which picture. It helps if the picture is to the left of or above its text.

3   Authentic information

I like a writer who is enthusiastic and committed to the particular subject. It is possible to write simply and yet accurately.

4   Illustrations which illustrate

I look for illustrations which complement and match the words rather than decorate the page. They should help a young reader to predict the text. Naturally, they should be accurate and clear.
NB Photographs are not always the easiest sort of illustration to interpret.

5   Characteristics of a good information book

I look for:
   Numbered pages
   Contents list
   Index.

6   Pointers ahead

I look for books with ideas for open-ended activities for the children and for bibliographies which will guide the children towards a wider knowledge of the subject.

Conclusion

The time is past when any writer with access to a reference book should feel that he or she can easily write an information book for children. It is a specialist job worthy of the same esteem we give to writers of 'children's literature'.

We should not teach our children that there are two kinds of books available in the library or book corner: stories that you read, and non-stories merely for looking at. They will begin to read information books seriously when we weed out the rubbish and give them books which are informed, lucid and enthusiastic.

Teaching children to use non-fiction books is interesting and rewarding. When they are very young, and learning to read, good non-fiction can be an effective addition to an individualized reading programme. As they get older, they like to collect everything from conkers to facts. A well-written information book gives great satisfaction and help in organizing their view of the world. As boys and girls leave the cosy surroundings of the primary school, we hope that they will realize that non-fiction books exist to serve them. It is our responsibility to give children the knowledge and skill to use them efficiently.

Questions to consider
1   What can a book offer which a film cannot?
2   What evidence is there that *all* the non-fiction books in your school get read sometimes?
3   How many of them have you actually read?
4   Can your children use an index and contents list properly?
5   Can the younger children use non-fiction books to consolidate and extend what they already know?
6   Can the older children distinguish between fact and opinion?
7   Can all the children find a clear and logical arrangement of information in the books provided for them?
8   Is there an adequate balance between fiction and non-fiction in your school? What should the proportion be?

Further reading

Fisher, M., *Matters of Fact*, Brockhampton, 1972.
Heeks, P., *Ways of Knowing*, Signal, 1982.
Meek, M., *Learning to Read*, Bodley Head, 1982.
Child Education and *Junior Education* published by Scholastic include topic-based booklists and regular non-fiction book reviews.

Acknowledgements

The photographs were taken by J. E. P. McKenzie.
I would like to thank the Head Teachers and children of Sunnymede Junior and Infant Schools for permission to quote their work.

Literature for primary children
Linnea Timson

Learning with literature

Literature as a vehicle for learning has enormous potential, with stories and poems providing an immediate resource of insights and experiences not otherwise available.

Donald Graves in *Writing: Teachers and Children at Work* makes a strong case for the value of literature in the classroom.

> The children need to hear, speak and read literature. Literature provides more than facts. It provides drama, problem solving, and precise language. Best of all, it is written by authors who know children and write with different voices than those usually found in text books. *Children's literature covers virtually the entire span of human experience and knowledge* [my emphasis].

Official sources have also stressed the importance of literature in learning. The Bullock Report, in Chapter 9 on literature, made the point that:

> In working his way through a book the reader imports, projects, anticipates, speculates on alternative outcomes; and *nowhere* is this process more active *than in a work of imaginative literature* [my emphasis] (9·11).

And seven years later in *Bullock Revisited*, Chapter 6, the HMIs are reporting that the chapter on literature deserves more attention than it seems to have received and that there is a need to:

> educate the teacher in an understanding of the nature of language and its part in human development; *and of the nature*, significance and operation of literature, and of allied media such as drama, in the larger context of language (6·9).

For the purposes of this chapter I have defined literature as: 'Poetic and fictional reading material which imaginatively engages the reader's attention in an interactive process which he or she considers either enjoyable or useful or both.'

One writer who seems to achieve this is Chris Powling. His story 'The Crimson Pirate', in *Daredevils or Scaredycats*, about three friends trying to go to the Saturday morning pictures, provides an example of the weedy under-sized boy who stands up to the over-sized bully. This enables primary children to learn that appearances can be deceptive.

> Sandra
>
> I think he's trying to say that a boy could be as small as a snail but have a temper of a boy the size of a gorilla.

> Brian
>
> The story shows that weeds can be strong underneath and bullies can be shown up.

> Claire
>
> I think the writer is trying to say that skinny people are not always shy, quiet and a scaredy cat.

Remembering their experience with Gene Kemp's *The Turbulent Term of Tyke Tyler*, where the reader wrongly attributes the sex of the main character, several pupils wanted to write to Chris Powling to check if each of the three friends in 'The Crimson Pirate' were actually boys. They had learnt they could no longer be certain of the sex of characters just from the way they behaved, and needed to see the sex of the character clearly stated.

Another story which can provide interesting insights is *The Shrinking of Treehorn* by F. P. Heide. In the story Treehorn, a schoolboy, starts to shrink but no one takes any notice of him. Like Bernard, in *Not Now Bernard*, Treehorn goes through his experience without anyone appreciating his predicament. This lack of sensitivity is often meted out to children, but, when slightly distanced in the story, it becomes an amusing and safe way to raise fundamental issues.

> The Shrinking of Treehorn – excerpts from a transcript
>
> *Anne:*   Can you read it again Miss?
>
> *Derek:*   He shrinks – the bus conductor thinks he's Treehorn's little brother – the Headmaster thinks there's no difference or he's mucking about.
>
> *Anne:*   Playing a game.
>
> *Brian:*   His mum is getting a bit worried thinking he might actually disappear.
>
> *Kate:*   She was more worried about the cake than about him. I bet the cake meant more'n him.
>
> *Teacher:*   Is anyone interested in the fact that he's shrinking?
>
> *Several pupils:*   Not really, Miss.
>
> *Kate:*   Except his dad *who was a bit annoyed.*
>
> *Derek:*   The teacher was a bit bothered about it . . . . *Nobody shrinks down here.*
>
> *Tracy:*   They think he's mucking about. They didn't believe what they saw.
>
> *Susan:*   They think he's doing a joke on them.
>
> *Kate:*   They knew though – they must just think . . . . It must be their imagination. He's in their imagination.
>
> *Susan:*   Startled perhaps.
>
> *Anne:*   They're like they're dreaming it all.

Using a novel for a project

John Cheetham makes a strong plea in 'Quarries in the Primary School' in G. Fox's *Writers, Critics and Children* for the use of a novel as a starting point for a project. *The Shrinking of Treehorn* could form an excellent starting point for a project on communication and relationships.

Some children feel that children are not treated seriously enough in books and are made to appear silly.

> Anne and Kate
>
> It's always about children –
> About children being silly.
> Why couldn't it be about grown ups?
> Grown ups can be silly too.

Treehorn shows the child as mature and the grown ups as silly. Art, drama and language work could examine this in depth.

Practical suggestions

1 Make a poster of Treehorn talking to his teacher.
2 Devise a comic strip recording the main incidents of his day.
3 Make models of Treehorn in various sizes.
4 Organize the improvisation of the interview with the Principal.
5 Organize the improvisation of action when teachers, parents or other children shrink.
6 Read and write stories about people who can change size at will.
7 Create a display called 'The Day I Shrank'.

This could develop into a range of activities related to giants, monsters and minute creatures, with the stories and poems written by the children being read and discussed alongside those of published authors.

What do the children like?

In organizing literature in the classroom, you need to be reasonably familiar with your pupils' tastes. Children's preferences do vary, but they also know more about books than adults normally assume. It is useful, therefore, to ask your class what they like, and to use this information when planning your programme. This can be done quite simply, and I would recommend using the two questions below, suggested to me by Margaret Meek, as the most effective for discovering children's real preferences.

1 What is the best book you have ever read?
2 Are there any books you have read more than once?

Here is eleven-year-old Philip's reply to the first question.

> It is very difficult to write about these books because I have read so many and a lot were good. Sometimes I read a book because of the mood I am in. Sometimes I read a war story then I would read a comic. As long as the book is exciting and does not go on I will read it. I like things that could be true but aren't.

Alice, a fourth year junior girl, complained:

> I wanted it about girls, because its always about boys, boys, boys. Books about boys are boring.

And Mary said:

> I always like the story where I can start off all scary and you get a real build-up — then it gets dense — you never know what happens but that makes you think about it. I really would like to know what Poker Face was — why was it the poker and what was wrong with him?
> ('Poker Face' story in Chris Powling's *Daredevils or Scaredycats.)*

Practical suggestions

Let the children:
1 make book jackets
2 choose characters to paint
3 illustrate scenes from books
4 *occasionally* write book reviews.

An easy format to use is shown below:

Book Review

Name of reader/reviewer:

Title of book:

Author:

What the book is about:

What I thought of the book:

What I thought of the pictures:

Talking about literature

The Assessment of Performance Unit (APU), in its Primary Survey Report No 1, *Language Performance in Schools*, found children much preferred *talking* about what they had read to writing about it.

> 70 per cent agreed with the statement
> 'I like talking about books I've read'.
> While only 40 per cent agreed with the statement
> 'I like writing about books I've read'.
> (p. 64)

A. N. Applebee in *The Child's Concept of Story* suggests that it is better for children to use their own choice of stories for discussion so that it is possible to:

> Look more directly at the meaning stories are given by the child, rather than at the process of giving meaning in the first place. (p. 91)

My experience in the classroom would confirm that where the poems and stories are *chosen* by the children the discussion is more fluent and extended than that where the material is chosen by the teacher.

Five things to do

A balloon debate

Have a balloon debate with three or more of the top favourite stories or poems in your classroom. Which one goes out first?

Desert island books

Which three or more books would you take with you as a castaway on a desert island?

A phone in programme

Geoff Fox in the periodical *Children's Literature in Education* suggests that you tape a simulated 'phone in' programme with 'calls' either to characters in the book, asking them about their actions, motives, etc, or to the author.

Interviews

One child interviews another about the story, poem or comic they've been reading.

Tape recorded discussions

If a tape recorder is used the children believe their opinions are being taken seriously and the teacher can learn from listening closely to the result. The child's half-formulated ideas are not lost and the record is invaluable.

Repetition and the multi-media approach

Literature can be read, listened to, seen on television, talked about or experienced in a combination of ways. From a close study of a group of primary children, I found that not only had all of them read some books twice, but they often chose to read for themselves books that had been presented in another form; and to present in another form, for example, through art or drama, a book they had already read.

The Shrinking of Treehorn was read to the children in assembly – they then asked for it to be read to them again. A number then chose to go on and read it for themselves and another group elected to improvise a play about the shrinking. The story has not vanished but has become an integral part of that class's culture.

Here, two children are discussing E. B. White's *Charlotte's Web*; one having seen it on television and the other having read it:

> *June:*   I know what the story reminds me of – it's *Charlotte's Web*. It's like when the pig had babies he was going to kill one of the babies 'cos it was more than the other one.
>
> *Derek:*   It's smaller.
>
> *June:*   That's what I said.
>
> *Derek:*   You said it's more than the other one.
>
> *June:*   More than. Oh did I? And Charlotte makes them grow up and that and get big.
>
> *Derek:*   And he makes a friend of the spider.

> *Peter aged 7 wrote*
>
> I like books after they have been read to me but not before because you don't know what the words are then.

> *Lucy aged 8 said*
>
> Miss Ball read it to me and I wanted to read it for myself.

Tracy's comment suggests she sees the value of dual presentation.

> If you know the characters like in *Grange Hill* you can really get into the book.

Further practical suggestions

1 *Feature an author a week*

Donald Graves describes a New Hampshire classroom where the teacher features *an author a week*. The author referred to is one of the children. The display includes a photograph of the *child* with a list of his or her writings, and a place for others to make comments. Information is also included about the child's favourite author, with questions posed about the characters from the stories for other children in the class to answer.

> Some children list books in order of preference, both with their own writing and the writing of their favourite author. Thus the child's own writing along with the writing of their favourite author is featured. (Graves, 1983, pp. 74–75)

2 *Integrate art work*

(a) Make a strip cartoon of a story or narrative poem.
(b) Make a frieze, model or map of any shared story, for example, Stevenson's *Treasure Island*, Terry Nation's *Rebecca's World*, or J. R. Tolkien's *The Hobbit*.
(c) Let the children draw any scene or character they choose — and use the resulting illustration as a starting point for telling a tale.

Poetry in the classroom

Poetry includes everything from limericks and nonsense to narrative and the serious. A good way, in my experience, of tackling poetry, is to integrate the reading and writing of poems all the time.

Read limericks and Spike Milligan's poems — then encourage the children to write something humorous. (The APU found that 82 per cent of children preferred reading 'funny poems to serious ones' — *Language Performance in Schools.*)

Read poems written by other children.

Let the children choose poems for reading and discussing.

Provide time for them to experiment with a variety of forms.

Sandy Brownjohn's *Does it Have to Rhyme?* is full of excellent practical suggestions.

Don't be apprehensive of becoming really involved in this most rewarding area. Many poems for children are short, so sessions need not be long.

Encourage individual children to read poems to you as an alternative to their reading book.

Let the whole class share *Matilda* by Belloc, or *The Owl and the Pussy Cat* by Lear, or a couple of poems by William Cole first thing in the morning, after break or during the last few minutes of a period.

Pupils writing poetry

I am an astronaut
And I am floating in space,
All on my own.
I can see the sun and I can see the stars.
And Saturn, a hundred thousand miles
From where I am.

▲

Poem by Hitendra   Illustrated by Paul

Creating a poem can be liberating because spelling and punctuation become less important. New words and sounds can be invented, and patterns made with shape poems.

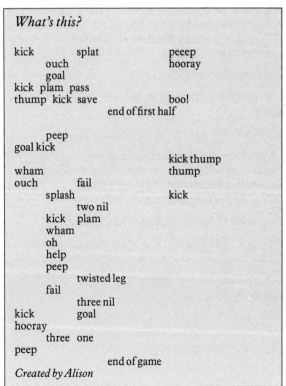

What's this?

```
kick        splat              peeep
    ouch                       hooray
    goal
kick plam pass
thump kick save                boo!
               end of first half

      peep
goal kick
                              kick thump
wham                          thump
ouch        fail
    splash                    kick
          two nil
    kick  plam
    wham
    oh
    help
    peep
          twisted leg
    fail
          three nil
kick      goal
hooray
      three one
peep
               end of game
Created by Alison
```

Try a brain pattern shape around a single idea.

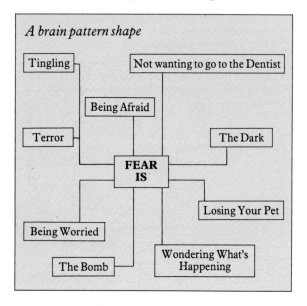

A brain pattern shape

Tingling — Not wanting to go to the Dentist — Being Afraid — Terror — The Dark — **FEAR IS** — Losing Your Pet — Being Worried — The Bomb — Wondering What's Happening

As more ideas and lines are generated a poem may be created, but it is the ideas and discussion that are important to start with. Children can choose some or all of the lines and sequence them as they choose — or try developing a poem using one of the lines as a title.

More ideas for getting started

Poems written *by* children are often far more accessible, particularly initially, to children who have little experience of poetry. One of the best collections of poems written by children is *Hey Mister Butterfly* edited by Alasdair Aston.

Read some to the class.

Let the children tell you which ones they want to hear again.

Let them copy out a favourite one and illustrate it.

Another useful collection of poems is *I Like This Poem* edited by Kaye Webb. All the poems were chosen by children and the book includes the reasons they gave for their choices.

Read some of the poems and the comments.

Encourage the children to discuss both the poems and the comments.

Suggest they choose poems they would include in a similar book.

Make an anthology of their choices.

Ways of encouraging children to write poems

Put up a piece of paper with a pencil attached and a title or first line like:

> My name is
>
> Silver is a shiny fish
>
> The Sea is a Cat
>
> The Glueblob stalks along the path
>
> There's a whale with a tale as strong as a hundred men

Pose ideas for a question and answer poem like:

> What is happiness?
>
> Happiness is . . . . . .
>
> What is yellow?
>
> Yellow is . . . .
>
> What is a pet?
>
> A pet is . . . .
>
> What is misery?
>
> Misery is . . . .
>
> What is school?
>
> School is . . . .

Literary collage

Some children may feel that they cannot cope with writing poetry. An interesting exercise is to encourage children to take lines from a variety of sources to create a poem for themselves. Whole or part lines can be taken from published poems, nursery rhymes, pop songs or even advertisements and sequenced to make a new poem. Here is an example.

> The year's at the Spring
> The rain is over and gone
> The time of the singing birds is come.
>
> Birds sing in tune
> To flowers of May
> But these are flowers that fly and sing
> All's right with the world.

The lines are taken from four poems in *I Like This Poem*. The first and last lines come from 'Pippa's Song', the intervening lines from other poems. Line 7 has two words omitted.

Making collages like this from already existing lines can be fun. It can also provide a way of giving children the confidence they need to try and write a poem by themselves.

Criteria for selection of literature

There is no infallible short cut to selecting books for children other than knowing the children and the books. However, reviews in the journals mentioned on page 61 can help. Some books are suitable for one or two children or a small group, others are wide enough in appeal to be enjoyed by the whole class.

However the material is used it should fulfil at least *one* of the following criteria.

1 *Does it extend the child's imagination?*

For example:
Sta'ar Kat by Andre Norton Knight.
The Hobbit by J. R. Tolkien.
The Colour Fairy Books by Andrew Lang.

2 *Does it have something clear and definite to say?*

For example:
Claire's Secret Ambition by Charlotte Firmin.
Panda's Puzzle by Michael Foreman.
Tusk, Tusk by David McKee.
Fair's Fair by Leon Garfield.
Johnny Tremain by Esther Forbes.
Nobody's Family's Going to Change by Louise Fitzhugh.

3 *Is it enjoyable and/or humorous?*

For example:
any Spike Milligan book.
Asterix books by Goscinny and Uderzo.
Funny Bones by Janet and Allan Ahlberg.
Help I'm a Prisoner in a Toothpaste Factory by John Antrobus.
The Trouble With Mum by Babette Cole.

4 *Does it have enough action to engage the primary child?*

For example:
The Treasure of Dubarry Castle by Lindsay Brown.
Rebecca's World by Terry Nation.
Daredevils or Scaredycats by Chris Powling.

5 *Is it well produced and a pleasure to experience?*

For example:
Joseph's Yard by Charles Keeping.
The Highwayman by Alfred Noyes (illustrated by Charles Keeping).
Story of Prince Rama by Brian Thompson.
Sunshine by Jan Ormerod.
Moonlight by Jan Ormerod.

6 *Has it succeeded in promoting a positive non-stereotyped picture of sex, race and class?*

For example:
Harriet the Spy by Louise Fitzhugh.
Mrs Plug the Plumber by Allan Ahlberg.
How We Feel, How We Work, and *How We Play* by Anita Harper and Christine Roche.

Useful resources

Open University Inset Pack P 530, Children, Language and Literature, 1982

This comprehensive pack includes a book on finding out about children's books, and a cassette which includes children reading and discussing stories and poems. The pack probably represents the single most useful resource for teachers.

Books

Fox, G. *et al., Writers, Critics and Children*
An excellent collection of articles from the first six years of the journal *Children's Literature in Education* (see page 62).

Grugeon, E., and Walden, P., *Literature and Learning*
Another perceptive collection of articles examining literature and learning from various perspectives most of which can be directly related to the primary school.

Writers, Critics and Children and *Literature and Learning* together provide an invaluable resource for teachers wanting to extend their use of literature with children.

Meek, M., Barton, G., and Warlow, A., *The Cool Web: the Pattern of Children's Reading*
A fascinating collection of articles not to be missed by the children's literature enthusiast.

Townsend, John Rowe, *An Outline History of English Literature Written for Children*
This revised edition of a book originally published in 1965 provides a useful history, within a single volume, of the development of children's literature. Details of many books and authors are included.

Journals

Books for Keeps 6 issues a year
Edited by Pat Triggs, 1 Effingham Road, Lee, London SE2 8NZ. The most lively and attractive of the reviewing journals.

Books for Your Children 3 issues a year
Edited by Anne Wood and Jean Russell, Slate House

Farm, Parwich, Nr Ashbourne, Derbyshire. Founded in 1965, the only journal written particularly for parents. Provides useful information for primary teachers, specially those who are less familiar with this area, or who are perhaps wanting to encourage greater parental involvement.

Children's Literature Abstracts quarterly
From C. H. Ray, Tan-y-Capel, Bont Dolgadfan, Llanbrynmair, Powys, SY19 7BB. An international abstracting journal, started in 1963, covering both fiction and non-fiction.

Children's Literature in Education quarterly
From Mrs B. E. M. Collinge, 2 Sunwine Place, Exmouth, Devon. This journal, which developed from the Exeter conferences on children's literature, provides serious in-depth cover on most aspects relating to children's literature in education.

The School Librarian quarterly
Journal of the School Library Association. Edited by Joan Murphy, SLA, Victoria House, 29–31 George Street, Oxford, OX1 2AY. A comprehensive journal containing reviews and articles covering the whole age-range. A must for any teacher with responsibility for either the library or book provision in the primary school.

Tried and Tested
Books to read to Infant and Junior classes annotated by ILEA teachers. From CLPE Ebury Teachers Centre, Sutherland Street, London SW1V 4LH. A small but most readable publication.

Poetry collections to use with children

Ahlberg, Allan, *Please Mrs Butler*.
Aston, Alasdair, *Hey Mr Butterfly*.
Belloc, Hilaire, *Selected Cautionary Verses*.
          More Beasts for Worse Children.
          Moral Alphabet.
Causley, Charles, *Figgie Hobbin*.
Cole, William, *Oh What Nonsense*.
          Oh That's Ridiculous.
          Oh How Silly.
          Beastly Boys and Ghastly Girls.
Ireson, Barbara, *The Faber Book of Nursery Verse*.
Lear, Edward, *The Owl and the Pussycat*.
          Book of Bosh, (ed. Brian Alderson).
          Complete Nonsense (ed. H. Jackson).
McGough, Roger, and Rosen, Michael, *You Tell Me*.
Milligan, Spike, *A Book of Milliganimals*.
          Silly Verse for Kids.
          Unspun Socks from a Chicken's Laundry.
          Milligan's Ark.
Rosen, Michael, *Wouldn't You Like to Know*.
          Mind Your Own Business.
Watson, Julia (ed.), *Children's Zoo: an Anthology of Animal Verse*.
Webb, Kaye (ed.), *I Like This Poem*.
Wright, Kit, *Hot Dog and Other Poems*.
          Rabbiting On.
Any other collection of poems *by* children you can find.

Further reading

Brownjohn, Sandy, *Does it Have to Rhyme? Teaching Children to Write Poetry*, Hodder and Stoughton, 1980.
          What Rhymes With Secret?, Hodder and Stoughton, 1982.

References and author index

Bold numbers indicate pages on which references occur

Agard, J., *Dig Away Two-Hole Tim*, Bodley Head, 1981 **37**

Ahlberg, Allan, *Please Mrs Butler*, Kestrel, 1983 **62**

  Mrs Plug the Plumber, Puffin, 1980 **61**

  Each Peach Pear Plum, Kestrel, 1978 **11**

Ahlberg, Janet and Allan, *Funny Bones*, Armada Lions, 1982 **61**

Andersen, H. C., *The Little Match Girl*, Kaye and Ward, 1981 **24**

Antrobus, John, *Help I'm a Prisoner in a Toothpaste Factory*, Knight Books, 1980 **61**

Applebee, A. N., *The Child's Concept of Story: Ages Two to Seventeen*, University of Chicago Press, 1980 **58**

Ashton-Warner, S., *Teacher*, Virago, 1980 **15**

Assessment of Performance Unit (APU), *Language Performance In Schools*, Primary Survey Report No. 1, HMSO, 1981 **3, 57, 59**

Aston, Alasdair (ed.), *Hey Mister Butterfly*, ILEA, 1978 **60, 62**

'BB', *The Little Grey Men*, Methuen **16**

Belloc, Hilaire, *Moral Alphabet*, Duckworth, 1974 **62**

  More Beasts for Worse Children, Duckworth, 1974 **62**

  Selected Cautionary Verses, Puffin, 1971 **62**

Bennett, Jill, *Learning to Read With Picture Books*, Signal Press, 1979 **2**

Berenstein, S. and J., *The Spooky Old Tree*, Collins, 1979 **11, 13**

  The Bear Scouts and other Bear books **19, 21**

  The Berenstain Bear's New Baby, Collins **21**

Big Books Series, Scholastic Publications **43**

Blake, Quentin, *Mister Magnolia*, Cape, 1980 **11**

Blyton, E., Secret Seven books **16, 25**

Bond, M., *Paddington's Garden*, Collins, 1972 **24**

Bonsall, C. N., *And I Mean It Stanley*, World's Work, 1979 **24**

Bradburne, E. S., *Early One Morning*, Schofield and Sims, 1971 **24**

Bridwell, N., *The Witch Next Door*, Scholastic **12, 24**

Briggs, Raymond, *Fungus the Bogeyman*, Hamish Hamilton 1977 **13**

  The Snowman, Hamish Hamilton, 1978 and Picture Puffins **13, 16, 24**

Brill, Edith, *The Golden Bird*, Puffin, 1974 **17**

Brown, Lindsay, *The Treasure of Dubarry Castle*, Hale, 1978, Piccolo, 1980 **61**

Brownjohn, Sandy, *Does It Have To Rhyme? Teaching Children to Write Poetry*, Hodder and Stoughton, 1982 **59, 62**

  What Rhymes with Secret?, Hodder and Stoughton, 1982 **62**

Bullock Report: *A Language for Life*, 1975 **1, 55**

Bullock Revisited, DES, 1982 **3, 7, 55**

Burningham, John, *The Snow*, Cape, 1974 **3**

  Would You Rather?, Cape, 1978 **12**

  Little Books, Cape **13**

Carle, E., *The Very Hungry Caterpillar*, Hamish Hamilton, 1970 **13**

Causley, Charles, *Figgie Hobbin*, Macmillan, 1979; Puffin, 1979 **62**

Centre for Urban Educational Studies, *Reading Through Understanding* (series) **44**

Chapman, L. J. and Czerniewska, P. (eds.), *Reading from Process to Practice*, Routledge & Kegan Paul, 1978 **11, 15**

Cheetham, J., 'Quarries in the Primary School', in Fox, G. *Writers, Critics and Children*, Heinemann Educational Books, 1976 **56**

Cole, Babette, *The Trouble With Mum*, Hamish Hamilton, 1983 **61**

Cole, William, *Oh What Nonsense*, Methuen, 1968 **62**

  Oh That's Ridiculous, Methuen, 1972 **62**

  Oh How Silly, Methuen, 1975 **62**

  Beastly Boys and Ghastly Girls, Methuen, 1971 (paper 1975) **62**

Dahl, R., *The Twits*, Puffin, 1982 **24**

Dickinson, M., *Alex's Outing*, Alex and Roy books, Deutsch, 1983 **37**

Dodd, M., *Merrymole the Magnificent*, Hodder and Stoughton, 1982 **24**

Donaldson, Margaret, *Children's Minds*, Fontana, 1978 **2**

Dumas, P., *Laura and the Bandits*, Fontana Lions, 1982 **24**

Eastman, P. D., *The Best Nest*, Collins, 1969 **20, 21**

Edwards, A. D. E., *Language in Culture and Class: the Sociology of Language and Education*, Heinemann Educational Books, 1976 **45**

Ellis, A. W., *British Fairy Tales*, Blackie, 1976, *Story Teller*, Marshall Cavendish, 1982 **24**

Ferreiro, Emilia and Teberosky, Ana, *Literacy Before Schooling*, Heinemann Educational Books, 1983 **3**

Firmin, Charlotte, *Claire's Secret Ambition*, Macmillan, 1972 **61**

Fisher, M., *Matters of Fact*, Brockhampton, 1972 **54**

Fitzhugh, Louise, *Nobody's Family's Going to Change*, Gollancz, 1976, Armada Lions, 1978 **61**

  Harriet the Spy, Gollancz, Armada Lions, 1975 **61**

Forbes, Esther, *Johnny Tremain*, Kestrel, 1974 **61**

Foreman, Michael, *Panda's Puzzle*, Hamish Hamilton, 1977 (paperback 1972) **61**

Fox, G., 'Twenty-four things to do with a book' in *Children's Literature in Education*, vol. 8, no. 3, 1975 **58**

Fox, G. *et al*, *Writers, Critics and Children*, Heinemann Educational Books, 1976 **56, 61**

Garfield, Leon, *Fair's Fair*, Macdonald, 1981 **61**

Goelman, H. *et al*, *Awakening to Literacy*, Heinemann Educational Books, 1984 **3**

Gollasch, F., *Language and Literacy: the collected writings of Kenneth S. Goodman*, vols 1 and 2, Routledge and Kegan Paul, 1982 **1, 2, 43**

Story Teller, Marshall Cavendish, 1982/1983 **24**

Teagles, A., *Casey the Utterly Impossible Horse*, Young Puffin **24**

Thomson, Brenda, *Learning to Read*, Sidgwick and Jackson, 1970 **2**

Thompson, Brian, *Story of Prince Rama*, Kestrel, 1980 **61**

Tolkien, J. R., *The Hobbit*, Unwin, 1981 **59, 61**

Tomlinson, J., *The Owl Who Was Afraid of the Dark*, Young Puffin **24**

Townsend, John Rowe, *An Outline History of English Literature Written for Children*, Penguin, 1983 **61**

Uttley, A., *Grey Rabbit and the Wandering Hedgehog*, Collins Colour Cubs, 1978 **24**

Walsh, J. P., *Babylon*, Deutsch, 1982 **37**

Watson, Julia (ed.), *A Children's Zoo: an Anthology of Animal Verse*, Armada Lions, 1978 **62**

Webb, Kaye (ed.), *I Like This Poem: Favourite Poems Chosen by Children*, Puffin, 1979 **60, 62**

Wells, Gordon, *Learning Through Interaction* (Bristol Language Development Project), CUP, 1981 **2**

White, E. B., *Charlotte's Web*, Hamish Hamilton, 1952; Puffin, 1969 **16, 58**

Williams-Ellis, Amabel, *British Fairy Tales*, 1976, *Story Teller*, Marshall Cavendish, 1982 **17, 24**

Wilson, N., *City Kids* (4 packs of 6 books in English plus Greek, Italian, Turkish, and no-text), Nelson **37**

Wright, Kit, *Hot Dog and Other Poems*, Puffin, 1982 **62**
       Rabbiting On, Armada Lion, 1978 **62**

Periodicals

Children's Literature in Education, vol. 8, no. 3, 1975, article by G. Fox **58**

English in Education, vol. 10, no. 1, 1976 (article by Margaret Spencer) **2**; vol. 16, no. 3, 1982 (article by Barrie Wade) **3**

The Guardian, 'Schoolbooks attacked for warped outlook on race' article by D. Kuya, 17 April, 1971 **45**

Subject index